Matin Latin II

STUDENT'S EDITION

by Karen L. Craig

Illustrated by Laura L. Blakey

Canon Press

Moscow, Idaho

Special Thanks to Charles, Darol, and David
without whose loving encouragement this project would not have been possible,
to Tabithah for practical help,
to Ron and Carol for hospitality,
to the administration at Logos School
for the opportunity to spend time writing these texts.

Karen L. Craig, *Matin Latin 2*

©1999 by Karen L. Craig
Published by Canon Press, P.O. Box 8741, Moscow, ID 83843
800-488-2034

Illustrations by Laura L. Blakey
Cover Design by Paige Atwood Design, Moscow, ID

Printed in the United States of America

ISBN: 1-885767-48-X

This book is dedicated to
Doug and Nancy with thanksgiving for their godly example.

Table of Contents

Matin Latin II

Preface

By choosing to study a second year of Latin you've indicated that the question "Why Latin?" has already been settled in your mind. You've seen, or are convinced of, the benefits of logical thinking skills, problem solving ability, vocabulary development, and syntax building. The challenge is to pass along the enjoyment of practical application of these benefits to your students. If Latin is merely another class in your daily schedule, students will develop a tolerance for that period of the day. Some will endure the time more cheerfully than others. However, if skills learned in other classes are used in Latin and skills learned in Latin are brought to other classes or better yet, into daily living, the time spent in the Latin text will be perceived as useful and may even come to be anticipated!

Mathematical skills may be reinforced in Latin study. Learning vocabulary is drill work quite similar to learning addition and multiplication facts. Reading or writing a Latin sentence closely resembles solving an equation for x, y, or z. Sometimes a Latin sentence will appear as a jigsaw puzzle. Music skills may be applied to learning the paradigms. The artistic side of life may be enhanced by encouraging students to picture the Latin story, the same as they would picture a story they read in English. Reading comprehension will be as much a part of Latin readings as it is of English readings. Original composition is the best method available for reviewing vocabulary and case and verb endings. Memorizing Latin poetry or scripture texts will sharpen the mind and create a storehouse of phrases for later use.

The exercises in this text have been written for variety. They certainly do not present an exhaustive resource for reviewing each lesson. By using several types of review tools or pattern drills, find the ones which best meet your students' needs and modify other drills to mimic the best ones for your students. *Beware* of the pitfall of verbatim translation. Although I have laboriously provided direct translations for the grammatical benefit of a deciphering teacher, the word-for-word method will slow down the pace of reading to a boring one at best and a time-consuming endurance contest at worst. Read sentence by sentence, paragraph by paragraph as you do in English. Then to reinforce grammar and to study style and syntax, go back over the selection at another time to parse the reading.

The beauty of language is that it is not simply mathematical, although Latin is very organized, but that there are musical qualities in the rhythm and flow of words and artistic qualities in the meanings and nuances associated with the choice of words. As you and your students become more familiar with the structure and vocabulary of Latin and English, may this new knowledge free you to express your ideas with a clarity unavailable to you before.

God, gods, goddesses, and myths

Nearly every people-group has a set of myths which mirror, although always with distortion, the biblical accounts of creation, the Flood, and natural phenomena in our world. The Sumerians' *Epic of Gilgamesh*, the Greek and Roman myths, Native American folklore, and African tales all attempt to explain the history of the world. Including some study of mythology gives background information about the culture and thought processes of a society. Even young students quickly distinguish between the facts of Scripture and the contrived explanations of storytellers blinded by godlessness (cf. I Chronicles 16:23–30).

As for the myriad gods and goddesses the Romans worshipped, even they may be explained from a study of Scripture. Many scholars believe that the "sons of God" in Genesis 6:1–4 were created beings whose offspring had superhuman characteristics and abilities. The Romans had no trouble accepting Romulus and Remus, founders of Rome, as having been twin sons of a Vestal Virgin, sired by the god Mars.

Throughout Scripture there are several instances of celestial or angelic beings participating in the affairs of men. Worshippers of the true God are distinguished from worshippers of idols, or false gods. The pagans believed that when they warred, their gods warred with them.[1] (See also I Samuel 4:1–10 and I Chronicles 10:8–14) In Daniel 10:12–14, the archangel Michael, spoken of as a chief prince, came to the aid of the unnamed lesser being who was also supernatural according to the description in verses 1–10. These two had a conflict with the "prince of the kingdom of Persia" (vss. 13, 20). Throughout the rest of the chapter, Daniel is helped by beings like men in appearance, but with superhuman abilities (Dan.10:15–21).

According to Ezekiel 28:1–19, the prince of Tyre and king of Tyre have set themselves against God and proclaimed themselves to be gods. Verses 15–19 make it clear that this being (king of Tyre from v. 12) was created and perfect (a supernatural characteristic) for a time. The word "cherub" refers to a "griffon," a terrifying-looking creature.[2] Psalm 86:8–.10 indicates that David accepted the idea of many gods but only one true God. I Chronicles 16:26 distinguishes between the gods of the people and the Lord who made the heavens and all the beings in them.

In the light of Scriptural truth, the myths of ancient peoples appear as the cheap imitations they are. Although one would not wallow in a study of the immoral deeds of these characters—gods, goddesses, demigods, or heathen men—these stories present valuable insights into the lives and thoughts of the people whose language (method of communication) one desires to comprehend.

[1]From *Savior of the World: A Series on Historical Optimism #2*, a sermon by Douglas Wilson, May 25, 1997.
[2]Ibid.

Suggested Memory Work

From Psalm 7

7:2 Domine Deus meus in te speravi salvum me fac ex omnibus persequentibus me et libera me

7:3 nequando rapiat ut leo animam meam dum non est qui redimat neque qui salvum faciat

7:4 Domine Deus meus si feci istud si est iniquitas in manibus meis

7:5 si reddidi retribuentibus mihi mala decidam merito ab inimicis meis inanis

7:6 persequatur inimicus animam meam et conprehendat et conculcet in terra vitam meam et gloriam meam in pulverem deducat diapsalma

From Psalm 19

18:2 caeli enarrant gloriam Dei et opera manuum eius adnuntiat firmamentum

18:3 dies diei eructat verbum et nox nocti indicat scientiam

18:4 non sunt loquellae neque sermones quorum non audiantur voces eorum

18:5 in omnem terram exivit sonus eorum et in fines orbis terrae verba eorum

18:6 in sole posuit tabernaculum suum et ipse tamquam sponsus procedens de thalamo suo exultavit ut gigans ad currendam viam suam;

18:7 a summo caeli egressio eius et occursus eius usque ad summum eius nec est qui se abscondat a calore eius

18:8 lex Domini inmaculata convertens animas testimonium Domini fidele sapientiam praestans parvulis

18:9 iustitiae Domini rectae laetificantes corda praeceptum Domini lucidum inluminans oculos

18:10 timor Domini sanctus permanens in saeculum saeculi iudicia Domini vera iustificata in semet ipsa

18:11 desiderabilia super aurum et lapidem pretiosum multum et dulciora super mel et favum

18:12 etenim servus tuus custodit ea in custodiendis illisretributio multa

18:13 delicta quis intellegit ab occultis meis munda me

18:14 et ab alienis parce servo tuo si mei non fuerint dominati tunc inmaculatus ero et emundabor a delicto maximo

18:15 et erunt ut conplaceant eloquia oris mei et meditatio cordis mei in conspectu tuo semper Domine adiutor meus et redemptor meus

Selections taken from the Textus Vulgatae Clementinae, the Latin translation of the Holy Bible, commonly known as the Vulgate.

Psalm 23

22:1 psalmus David Dominus reget me et nihil mihi deerit

22:2 in loco pascuae ibi; me conlocavit super aquam refectionis educavit me

22:3 animam meam convertit deduxit me super semitas iustitiae propter nomen suum

22:4 nam et si ambulavero in medio umbrae mortis non timebo mala quoniam tu mecum es virga tua et baculus tuus ipsa me consolata sunt

22:5 parasti in conspectu meo mensam adversus eos qui tribulant me inpinguasti in oleo caput meum et calix meus inebrians quam praeclarus est

22:6 et misericordia tua subsequitur me omnibus diebus vitae meae et ut inhabitem in domo Domini in longitudinem dierum

Psalm 24

23:1 psalmus David prima sabbati Domini est terra et plenitudo eius orbis terrarum et universi; qui habitant in eo

23:2 quia; ipse super maria fundavit eum et super flumina praeparavit eum

23:3 quis ascendit in montem Domini aut quis stabit in loco sancto eius

23:4 innocens manibus et mundo corde qui non accepit in vano animam suam nec iuravit in dolo proximo suo

23:5 hic accipiet benedictionem a Domino et misericordiam a Deo salvatore suo

23:6 haec est generatio quaerentium eum quaerentium faciem Dei Iacob diapsalma

23:7 adtollite portas principes vestras et elevamini portae aeternales et introibit rex gloriae

23:8 quis est iste rex gloriae Dominus fortis et potens Dominus potens in proelio

23:9 adtollite portas principes vestras et elevamini portae aeternales et introibit rex gloriae

23:10 quis est iste rex gloriae Dominus virtutum ipse est rex gloriae diapsalma

An alphabetic phonics chart looks like this (to alleviate pronunciation difficulties, in the English examples phonetic symbols from Webster's New Collegiate Dictionary were used):

Vowels					
Long	Latin	English	Short	Latin	English
ā	irāta, lāta	father	a	casa	banana, but
ē	poēta, rēs, tē	date, day, they	e	et, est	bet, met
ī	prīma, vīlla	beet, easy	i	in, inter	in, pin
ō	Rōma, sōla	bone, no	o	bona, nova	obey, omit
(ō and o are very similar)					
ū	fortūna, lacūna	food, loot, lute	u	sub, sunt	foot, full, put
Diphthongs					
ae	puellae, tubae	aisle, eye			
au	aut, nauta	out, pouch			
(Infrequent dipthongs are included here only for reference: <u>ei</u> as in n<u>ei</u>ghbor and w<u>ei</u>gh; <u>oe</u> as in <u>oy</u> in b<u>oy</u>, j<u>oy</u>; <u>eu</u> as in f<u>eu</u>d, and f<u>ew</u>; <u>ui</u> as in q<u>u</u>een.)					

Consonants			
b, d, f, h, k, l, m, n, p, qu, r sound the same in Latin and in English		s	as in *say*
bs and **bt**	have a soft sound like *ps* and *pt*	t	as in *ton*
c and **ch**	always hard as in *character*	th	as in *thyme* or *thick* (not as in *then*)
g	always hard as in *go*	ti	as in *tin* (does **not** combine as in *nation*)
gu	as in *anguish*	v	always sounds like *w* as in *wall*
i (j)	begins a word and is followed by a vowel; sounds like *y* in *yam*	x	always sounds like *ks* as in *axe* (double consonant)
ph	as in *photograph*	z	always sounds like *dz* as in *adze* (double consonant)

The syllabification of Latin words

Dividing into syllables and placing an accent makes a word easier to pronounce.

A. Each vowel or diphthong has its own syllable.

B. Consonants are pronounced with the following vowel. Two consonants are divided and one pronounced with each vowel.

C. Consonant blends: *h, l,* and *r* combine with a preceding *c, g, p, b, d,* or *t* to form a blend which is pronounced with the following vowel.

D. When *u* follows *g, q,* and sometimes *s,* it sounds like *w* and forms a blend which is pronounced with the following vowel.

E. Double consonants: *x* is pronounced with the preceding vowel, *z* is pronounced with the following vowel.

F. The last syllable of a Latin word is the *ultima,* the next to last is the *penult,* and the one before that is the *antepenult.*

Accents

In words of more than one syllable, the ultima is never accented. (*This rule is ignored during Practice Chants.*) If the penult is long (it has a long vowel or is followed by two or more consonants), it is accented. If the penult is short, the accent will be on the antepenult. Simply stated, *if the next to last syllable is long, it is accented. If the next to last syllable is short, the syllable which precedes it receives the accent.*

Lesson One

In this lesson we will review the noun cases which we have already learned.

A noun is the name of a person, place, thing, or idea. *Girl, boy, forest, water,* and *friendship* are all nouns. Can you name some other nouns? Nouns which tell who or what is doing the action of the sentence are called *subject* nouns, or the *subject* of the sentence. In Latin the subject of a sentence uses the nominative case.

A predicate nominative renames the subject after a linking verb. A predicate nominative also uses the nominative case.

A noun which shows possession (the *girl's* coat) uses the genitive case in Latin.

A noun which shows *to whom* or *for whom* the action of the verb was done is called the indirect object. In Latin the indirect object uses the dative case.

A noun which receives the action of a verb is the direct object. In Latin a direct object uses the accusative case.

A noun which is the object of a preposition uses the accusative or the ablative case in Latin. The case of this noun depends on the preposition and the meaning in the sentence.

CASE	SINGULAR	PLURAL
Nominative	puell*a*	puell*ae*
Genitive	puell*ae*	puell*ārum*
Dative	puell*ae*	puell*īs*
Accusative	puell*am*	puell*ās*
Ablative	puell*ā*	puell*īs*

Lesson One Exercises

A. Underline the subject in these sentences.

 1. The boys sail.

 2. The slaves walk.

 3. Men call.

 4. Horses work.

 5. A messenger tells.

 6. Agricolae ambulant.

 7. Poēta nārrat.

 8. Nautae nāvigābant.

 9. Famulae labōrābit.

 10. Bēstiae vocābant.

B. Underline the predicate nominative and circle the direct object in these sentences.

 1. Fido is a puppy.

 2. The owl caught a mouse.

 3. The puppy has a bone.

 4. My cat is a Persian.

 5. The cow eats corn.

 6. Unda nāviculam portat.

 7. Fīlia fēmina est.

8. Umbrae ursam cēlābant.

9. Silva cūrās ēvocat.

10. Figūrae deae sunt.

C. Circle the indirect object and underline phrases (groups of words) which show possession. Some sentences will not be marked.

1. God gave Adam a garden.

2. Adam's garden gave Adam and Eve fruit.

3. God told Adam the rules of the garden.

4. Adam obeyed God's rules for a time.

5. Then the serpent told Eve a lie.

6. Bēstia fēminae fābulam dabat.

7. Fābula bēstiae fāma mala erat.

8. Fēmina bēstiam nōn culpābat.

9. Tum fēmina herbam dēsīderābat.

10. Deus (God) fēminae poenam nārrat.

D. Tell the object of the preposition. For the Latin sentences tell the case of the noun.

1. Galba and Silvanus are walking on the seashore.
2. Today the waves are quiet, but pirates are on a nearby island.
3. Galba lives near the coast.
4. Silvanus is a farmer and does not live near the sea.
5. His villa is near high Aetna.
6. Galba vīllam prope Aetnam spectat et fābulam nārrat.
7. "Olim ambulābam in ōrā.
8. Pīrātās cum gemmīs spectābam.
9. Pīrātae in terrā gemmās cēlābant.
10. Tum pīrātās in ōrā nōn dēsīderō!"

E. Review the Latin noun vocabulary from Book One.

DAILY ORAL REVIEW

Complete these sentences:

A noun is

A pronoun takes the place of

A predicate nominative renames

An indirect object shows

A direct object

Lesson Two

Verbs tell the action of the subject. Verbs have tense—the time that the action happened.

The present tense tells that the action is happening now.

The imperfect tense tells what used to happen or was happening over a long period of time before now.

The future tense tells what will happen in the future, sometime after right now.

Action verbs may have a pronoun (I, you, he, she, it; we, you, they) for a subject. They may also have a direct object.

Linking verbs are different. They do not tell action. They link two parts of the sentence that are the same. A linking verb has a subject and a predicate nominative or a predicate adjective. A linking verb is also called a "state of being verb." The forms of "to be," *is, are, was, were, will be* are easy to identify. Other verbs like *seems, appears, looks,* are also linking verbs.

The infinitive is also a special kind of verb. *To* plus a verb is called the *infinitive. To play, to run,* and *to be* are all infinitives.

Lesson Two Exercises

A. Label the verb P(Present), I(Imperfect), or F(Future) to show the tense.

_____ 1. Long ago, many men were doing bad deeds.

_____ 2. Noah is a good man.

_____ 3. Noah will build a huge boat for his family.

_____ 4. His family is helping Noah with the ark.

_____ 5. It was taking a long time to build.

_____ 6. Noe et familia in arcā habitant.

_____ 7. Multae aquae in terrā erunt.

_____ 8. Tum multae undae super terram arcam portābant.

_____ 9. Arca super undās et aquās familiam conservābit.

_____ 10. Nunc vīta in terrā nōn erat, sed Noe et familia in terrā habitābant.

B. Underline the action verbs, circle the linking verbs, and draw a box around the infinitives. Some sentences have more than one verb.

1. Noah and his sons were the fathers of all people on the earth.
2. Everyone spoke the same language.
3. Many people lived on a plain in the land of Shinar.
4. They decided to build a tower to reach the sky.
5. God was not pleased when he saw the tower.
6. He gave the people many different languages.
7. They did not understand each other.
8. They stopped the building of the tower.
9. Then they found others who spoke their language.
10. Each group moved away to different parts of the earth.

C. Review the Latin verb vocabulary from Book One.

Lesson Three

Latin verbs have four principal parts. The first principal part tells the first person, present form. The second principal part is the infinitive. When it is used by itself it means "*to* plus a verb." But more importantly, this principal part is used to form the three simple tenses (present, imperfect, future) of a verb.

> Infinitive – *re* = present stem

> Present tense = present stem + personal endings

Present

SINGULAR		PLURAL	
vocō	I call	vocā*mus*	we call
vocā*s*	you call	vocā*tis*	you (pl.) call
voca*t*	he, she, it calls	voca*nt*	they call

> # Imperfect tense =
> ## present stem + tense sign + personal endings

IMPERFECT

vocā*bam*	I was calling	vocā*bāmus*	we were calling
vocā*bās*	you were calling	vocā*bātis*	you were calling
vocā*bat*	he, she, it was calling	vocā*bant*	they were calling

> # Future tense =
> ## present stem + tense sign + personal endings

FUTURE

vocā*bō*	I will call	vocā*bimus*	we will call
vocā*bis*	you will call	vocā*bitis*	you will call
vocā*bit*	he, she, it will call	vocā*bunt*	they will call

Review the verb *sum* in the present, imperfect, and future tenses.

PRESENT

sum	I am	*sumus*	we are
es	you are	*estis*	you (pl.) are
est	he, she, it is	*sunt*	they are

IMPERFECT

eram	I was	*erāmus*	we were
erās	you were	*erātis*	you (pl.) were
erat	he, she, it was	*erant*	they were

FUTURE

erō	I will be	*erimus*	we will be
eris	you will be	*eritis*	you (pl.) will be
erit	he, she, it will be	*erunt*	they will be

Lesson Three Exercises

A. Write the correct Latin verb.

1. amō: 1st person, singular, present tense _____

2. ambulō: 2nd person, plural, imperfect _____

3. cēlō: 3rd person, singular, future _____

4. clāmō: 1st person, plural, imperfect _____

5. errō: 3rd person, plural, present _____

6. sum: 1st person, plural, imperfect _____

7. iuvō: 2nd person, singular, future _____

8. laudō: 2nd person, plural, present _____

9. nāvigō: 3rd person, singular, future _____

10. sum: 2nd person, singular, present _____

B. Tell the English subject pronoun for each of the verbs in exercise A.

C. Rewrite this paragraph using all future tense verbs. Do not change *inquit* or *inquiunt*.

Ad nautārum casās properat. Nautārum fīliae perterritae, "Cum pīrātīs," inquiunt, "est Iūlia tua." Magna est īra agricolae. Galeam et hastam raptat. Nautae nāviculam suam agricolae dant. Nautae quoque galeās et hastās raptant, et cum agricolā ad pīrātārum nāviculam properant. Tum agricola pīrātās vocat, "Ubi," inquit, "est fīlia mea?" Pīrātae, "Fīlia tua," inquiunt, "in nāviculā nostrā est." Tum agricola pecūniam multam pīrātīs dat. Pīrātae Iūliam ad agricolae nāviculam portant.

D. Review the Latin verbs from Book One.

E. Study these new Latin words.

īra, -ae, f.   porta, -ae, f.   properō, -āre, -āvī, -ātum

cēna, -ae, f.	supper
tabula, -ae, f.	tablet
tunica, -ae, f.	tunic
exclāmō, -āre, -āvī, -ātum	to exclaim, to cry out
raptō, -āre, -āvī, -ātum	to snatch, to seize
recitō, -āre, -āvī, -ātum	to read aloud, to recite

DAILY ORAL REVIEW

Chant the noun paradigm using a different noun each day.

Conjugate a verb in the present, imperfect, and future tenses.

Lesson Four

An adjective modifies (describes) a noun or pronoun.

In Latin an adjective agrees with the noun it modifies in gender, number, and case. So far we have only learned the feminine gender, which is the middle form in a dictionary listing of the adjective.

An adjective answers the questions
which one?, what kind?, how many?
about a noun or pronoun.

A preposition is a short word which tells the relationship of a noun to other parts of the sentence. In book one we learned about Prep, the frog, and his position in relation to his box. He could be *in* the box, *on* the box, *over* the box, etc.

Lesson Four Exercises

A. Underline the adjectives. Draw an arrow to the noun which is being modified.

1. Abraham was an old man who served God.
2. He wanted his only son, Isaac, to have a good wife.
3. He sent his servant Eliezer to find a lovely wife.
4. Eliezer and several men took ten camels to Nahor, a distant country.
5. The tired, thirsty camels knelt beside a deep well of cool water.
6. Puella pulchra aquam portat.
7. Eliezer aquam grātam rogābat.
8. Puella pulchra camelīs altīs aquam grātam dabat.
9. Tum Eliezer puellam grātam laudābat.
10. Puella grāta, bona, et pulchra Isaac erit.

B. Study these new adjectives.

extrēmus, extrēma, extrēmum	extreme, farthest
parātus, parāta, parātum	ready, prepared
perterritus, perterrita, perterritum	terrified, frightened
splendidus, splendida, splendidum	splendid

COLORS

albus, alba, album	white
caeruleus, caerulea, caeruleum	blue
croceus, crocea, croceum	orange
flavus, flava, flavum	yellow
fuscus, fusca, fuscum	brown
niger, nigra, nigrum	black
purpureus, purpurea, purpureum	purple
ruber, rubra, rubrum	red

C. Give five English derivatives from the Latin adjectives.

D. Underline the prepositional phrases (the preposition and the noun or pronoun that follows, plus any words between them). Use a stilum croceum. (A stilus (-ī, m.) is a writing stick.)

1. In a small cottage near a large forest lived a lazy ant.

2. In summer the ant carried food into her house.

3. Near the ant's house lived a lazy grasshopper.

4. He always sang, but he didn't carry food into his house.

5. In winter the ant had food; the grasshopper had no food on his table.

6. Cicāda (grasshopper) ad casam formīcae (ant) volat; januam pulsat.

7. Per fenestram formīca cicādam spectat.

8. "Cibum dēsīderō!" cicāda inquit (says). Per januam clāmat.

9. In mensā formīcae cibum est quod (because) formica labōrābat cum (when) cicāda cantābat.

10. Cicāda quiēta ā casā formīcae volat; nōn iam cantat.

F. Review the Latin prepositions from Book One.

ā, ab (ablative) *away from*
ad (accusative) *to, toward*

circum (accusative) *around*
cum (ablative) *with*

dē (ablative) *concerning, about*
ē, ex (ablative) *away from*

in (accusative) *into*
in (ablative) *in, on*
inter (accusative) *between, among*

per (accusative) *through*
post (accusative) *after, behind*
prō (ablative) *in front of, for, on behalf of*
prope (accusative) *near*

DAILY ORAL REVIEW

Complete these sentences:

An adjective answers the questions

A preposition tells

Lesson Five

Latin has five noun declensions. We have already learned many first declension nouns. Most of the first declension nouns are feminine in gender.

Now we will learn the second declension noun paradigms. There is a paradigm for the masculine nouns and one for the neuter nouns. These paradigms are very much alike, so they both belong to the second declension.

Here is the second declension masculine noun paradigm.

CASE	SINGULAR	PLURAL
Nominative	amīc*us*	amīc*ī*
Genitive	amīc*ī*	amīc*ōrum*
Dative	amīc*ō*	amīc*īs*
Accusative	amīc*um*	amīc*ōs*
Ablative	amīc*ō*	amīc*īs*

Most second declension masculine nouns end in *-us* in the nominative form. There are a few which end in *-r* or *-er*. These will have the genitive form given in the text listing so that the stem will be easy to find. (*liber, librī*, m.; *magister, magistrī*, m.)

> To find the stem of a noun, drop the ending from the genitive singular form.

A few nouns keep the -e- of the nominative form (*puer, puerī,* m.; *vesper, vesperī,* m.), but the declension endings are the same as for the -*us* nouns.

Here is the paradigm for words like *puer, puerī, m.–boy.*

CASE	SINGULAR	PLURAL
Nominative	puer	puerī
Genitive	puerī	puerōrum
Dative	puerō	puerīs
Accusative	puerum	puerōs
Ablative	puerō	puerīs

English derivatives of -*r* and -*er* nouns give clues to their Latin stem: library, magistrate, puerile, vespers.

Lesson Five Exercises

A. Study this new vocabulary. Remember to learn the entire Latin entry for each word.

ager, agrī, m.

annus, annī, m.

lūdus, lūdī, m.

magister, magistrī, m.

puer, puerī, m.

amīcus, amīcī, m.	friend
angulus, angulī, m.	corner
iuvencus, iuvencī, m.	bullock
liber, librī, m.	book

B. Chant the second declension masculine paradigm using a different noun each day.

Monday—ager, agrī

Tuesday—lūdus, lūdī

Wednesday—annus, annī

Thursday—magister, magistrī

Friday—angulus, angulī

C. Give the Latin word from which we get each English word.

1. agriculture   _____

2. amicable   _____

3. ludicrous   _____

4. library

5. annual _____

6. angle _____

7. magistrate _____

Challenge: Use each of these words in a sentence which shows its meaning.

_____

_____

_____

_____

_____

_____

_____

_____

_____

D. Draw pictures or write a good English sentence to show the meaning of these Latin sentences.

1. Puer in angulō stābat.   2. Magister puerō librum dat.

3. Iuvencī nigrī in agrōs errant.　　4. Puerī lūdōs amābunt.

5. Magistrī puerīs et puellīs fābulās in lūdum nārrant.

6. Amīcī puerī cum iuvencīs blancīs nōn labōrābunt.

Lesson Six

The declension of second declension neuter nouns looks very much like the masculine nouns' declension. Notice that the nominative and accusative singular are alike and the nominative and accusative plural are alike. Neuter nouns of the second declension end in *-um* in their nominative singular form.

Here is the second declension neuter noun paradigm.

CASE	SINGULAR	PLURAL
Nominative	for*um*	for*a*
Genitive	forī	forōrum
Dative	forō	forīs
Accusative	for*um*	for*a*
Ablative	forō	forīs

All neuter nouns in Latin have the same form for both nominative and accusative. The neuter plural forms always end with *-a*.

Lesson Six Exercises

A. Study this new vocabulary. Remember to learn the entire Latin entry for each word.

benignus, benigna, benignum

caelum, caelī, n.

industrius, industria, industrium

dōnum, dōnī, n.

longinquus, longinqua, longinquum

oppidum, oppidī, n.

piger, pigra, pigrum

proelium, proeliī, n.

forum, forī, n.	forum
impavidus, impavida, impavidum	fearless
nullus, nulla, nullum	no, none
plaustrum, plaustrī, n.	wagon
prandium, prandiī, n.	lunch, dinner

B. Say or write the chant for:

cēna

ager

donum

C. Read the story and underline all the second declension nouns.

Laeta est Iūlia quod iterum casam parvam cum agricolā habitat. Sed Iūlia puella duodecim annōrum iam est. Itaque agricola fīliae suae tabulās dat. Pecūniam quoque lūdī magistrō dat. Cotīdiē puella ad lūdum per agrōs ambulat. Multī iuvēncī in agrōs sunt, sed impavida est puella. Tabulās ad lūdum Iūlia portat. In tabulās litterae multae sunt. Lūdī magister Iūliam laudat quod litterās bene cotīdiē recitat. In lūdō multī puerī, multae puellae cum Iūliā sunt. Magister lūdum bene gubernat. Industriīs puerīs magister librōs pulchrōs dat; pigrōs malōsque puerōs nōn laudat sed culpat. Magna est īra magistrī quod puerī pigrī litterās nōn bene recitant. Itaque puerī pigrī in angulīs stant. Multae sunt lacrimae puerōrum malōrum. Itaque puerī industriī sunt et litterās bene recitant. Iūlia prandium ad lūdum cotīdiē portat, quod longa est via. In agrōs prandium est Iūliae grātum.

Multās fābulās puerīs et puellīs magister benignus in lūdō nārrat nunc dē Britanniā, nunc dē longinquās terrās fābulās nārrat. Grātae puerīs et puellīs sunt fābulae. Nunc igitur in librō nōn sōlum Iūliae sed multīs etiam puerīs et puellīs fābulās nārrō.

Vocabulary:
bene, adv.—well
cotīdiē, adv.—every day
dē, prep. with abl.—down from, concerning, about
duodecim—twelve
etiam, adv.—even, also
iam, adv.—now, already, by this time
nōn iam, adv.—no longer

nunc, adv.—now, at this time
igitur, adv.—therefore

itaque, conj.—and so, therefore
per, prep. with acc.—through, among
-que—and (attached to the end of a word)
sōlum, adv.—only

D. Answer these questions about the story using good Latin sentences.

    1. Why does Julia's father give her tablets?

    2. Where does Julia take the tablets?

    3. Why is Julia praised?

    4. What happens to lazy boys in this school?

    5. Why does Julia carry a lunch to school?

    6. What kind of stories will be in this book?

Lesson Seven

In the story in lesson six, we had a new construction! A *construction* in Latin is the use of a case for a particular reason. Look at these sentences from the story.

In agrīs prandium est Iūliae grātum.

Grātae puerīs et puellīs sunt fābulae.

What case is used for *Iūliae*, *puerīs*, and *puellīs*? It is the dative case. This use of the dative is called the *dative with adjectives*. With adjectives like *grātus (pleasing)*, *benignus (kind)*, *amīcus (friendly)*, *propinquus (near)*, which often carry the meaning *to*, the dative case is used. In the sentences above, the lunch is pleasing (to) Julia; the stories are pleasing (to) the boys and girls.

The story also had many masculine nouns which had adjectives to modify them. Here are some examples.

multī puerī

industriīs puerīs

librōs pulchrōs

puerī pigrī

puerōrum malōrum

How are these adjectives different from the ones we've used before? They have masculine endings because they are modifying masculine nouns.

> ## Adjectives agree with the nouns they modify in gender, number, and case.

Adjectives which modify neuter nouns would have neuter endings. Here are examples of neuter nouns and their adjectives.

oppidum longinquum

magnō forō

nulla dona

prandiīs bonīs

We have learned only two declensions of nouns and adjectives. Therefore many times the ending of an adjective will be the same as the ending of the noun it modifies. *However*, do not rely on this sameness to identify them. An adjective agrees with the noun it modifies in gender, number, and case . . . even when they don't look alike.

Think about how we would talk about a good farmer. What would the nominative noun look like? What would the nominative adjective look like? Would they have the same ending? *Agricola bonus* would be the correct way to write the nominative form. The endings do not *look* alike, but they are the same gender (masculine), number (singular), and case (nominative).

Lesson Seven Exercises

A. Fill in the paradigm for a complete declension of the adjective *bonus*. Some of the spaces have been filled for you.

SINGULAR

	MASCULINE	FEMININE	NEUTER
Nominative	bonus	bona	bonum
Genitive	bonī		
Dative		bonae	
Accusative			bonum
Ablative			

PLURAL

	MASCULINE	FEMININE	NEUTER
Nominative	bonī	bonae	bona
Genitive			bonōrum
Dative		bonīs	
Accusative	bonōs		
Ablative	bonīs		

B. Decline (orally):

fēmina benigna

magnus angulus

caelum rubrum

nauta impavidus

C. Study this new vocabulary.

aedificō, -āre, -āvī, -ātum	to build
arō, -āre, -āvī, -ātum	to plow
Britannus, Britannī, m.	a Briton
clīvus, clīvī, m.	hill
equus, equī, m.	horse
Italia, Italiae, f.	Italy
Italus, Italī. m.	an Italian
oculus, oculī, m.	eye
olīva, olīvae, f.	olive
oppidānus, oppidānī, m.	townsman
placidus, placida, placidum	calm
rectus, recta, rectum	straight, right
Rōmānus, Rōmāna, Rōmānum *(adj.)*	Roman
ūva, ūvae, f.	grape
validus, valida, validum	strong
vīnea, vīneae, f.	vineyard

D. Use a dictionary, if needed, to find the origin and meaning of these English words.

1. equestrienne _____

2. oculomotor nerve _____

3. vineyard _____

4. edify _____

5. arable _____

E. Read this story.

ITALIA

Caeruleum est Italiae caelum. Italī caelum caeruleum amant. Britannīs quoque caelum caeruleum grātum est, sed nōn saepe Britanniae caelum caeruleum est. Italiae agricolae olivās et ūvās laudant, iuvēncīs albīs agrōs arant. Placidī sunt oculī iuvēncōrum. Placidī et pulchrī sunt iuvēncī. Italiae agricolīs grātī sunt iuvēncī. Britannicī agricolae nōn iuvēncīs sed equīs agrōs arant. Validī et pulchrī sunt, equī magnī.

In Italiā clīvī multī sunt. Italiā in clīvīs parvīs oppida aedificant. Oppïdānī oppida in clīvīs habitant. In campō vīneae et olīvae sunt in clīvīs, oppida. Per campōs viae Rōmānae sunt. Longae et rectae sunt viae Rōmānae. Oppidānī olīvīs et ūvās, agricolae pecūniam dēsīderant. Itaque oppidānī pecūniam agricolīs dant, et per viās Rōmānās agricolae olīvās et ūvās ad oppida in plaustrīs portant.

F. Draw three pictures from the story above:

1) Show the British farmers in their fields.

2) Show the Italian farmers in their fields.

3) Show the townspeople and the farmers of Italy.

G. Conjugate *saltō* in the present, imperfect, and future tenses.

DAILY ORAL REVIEW

An adjective agrees with the noun it modifies in gender, number, and case.

Optional Unit – Numbers

Numerals are adjectives; they tell *how many*. Most of them, however, are indeclinable. This makes them quite easy to use in sentences and for daily activities.

The cardinal numerals are the counting numbers. *Unus, duo,* and *trēs* are declined.

The ordinal numerals tell order (first, second, third), and they are declined like *bonus, -a, um.*

Here are the paradigms for *ūnus, duo,* and *trēs.*

	MASCULINE	FEMININE	NEUTER
SINGULAR			
Nominative	ūnus	ūna	ūnum
Genitive	ūnīus	ūnīus	ūnīus
Dative	ūnī	ūnī	ūnī
Accusative	ūnum	ūnam	ūnum
Ablative	ūnō	ūnā	ūnō
PLURAL			
Nominative	duo	duae	duo
Genitive	duōrum	duārum	duōrum
Dative	duōbus	duābus	duōbus
Accusative	duōs	duās	duo
Ablative	duōbus	duābus	duōbus

	MASCULINE/FEMININE	NEUTER
Nominative	trēs	tria
Genitive	trium	trium
Dative	tribus	tribus
Accusative	trēs	tria
Ablative	tribus	tribus

ROMAN NUMERALS

	CARDINAL	ORDINAL
I	ūnus, -a, -um	prīmus
II	duo, duae, duo	secundus
III	trēs, trēs, tria	tertius
IV	quattuor	quārtus
V	quīnque	quīntus
VI	sex	sextus
VII	septem	septimus
VIII	octō	octāvus
IX	novem	nōnus
X	decem	decimus
XI	ūndecim	ūndecimus
XII	duodecim	duodecimus
XIII	tredecem	tertius decimus
XIV	quattuordecim	quārtus decimus
XV	quīndecim	quīntus decimus
XVI	sēdecim	sextus decimus
XVII	septendecim	septimus decimus
XVIII	duodēvīgintī	duodēvīcēsimus
XIX	ūndēvīgintī	ūndēvīcēsimus
XX	vīgintī	vīcēsimus
L	quīnquāgintā	
C	centum	
M	mīlle	

Lesson Eight

In this lesson we will learn another part of a sentence, the adverb. An adverb modifies a verb, an adjective, or another adverb.

An adverb answers the questions
how? when? where? how much?
about a verb, an adjective, or another adverb.

Adverbs in English often (but not always) end in *-ly*. *Quickly, happily,* and *suddenly* are all adverbs. Words like *high, there,* and *very* are adverbs, too.

Sometimes the same word can have different uses in sentences. For example, in the following sentences *high* is used as an adjective or an adverb.

The bear was on a high branch. (adjective)

The high jump bar is missing. (adjective)

The bear is high in the tree. (adverb)

High in the sky is a small cloud. (adverb)

Sometimes we can tell that an adverb was made from an adjective. By adding *-ly* to these adjectives we create adverbs: *slow (slowly), strong (strongly), certain (certainly), sure (surely), loud (loudly), large (largely), near (nearly).*

Lesson Eight Exercises

A. Underline the adverbs and draw arrows to the words they modify. Use a stilum purpureum.

1. Isaac and Rebekah lived happily together.
2. They greatly desired to have children.
3. Isaac prayed very earnestly to God.
4. Soon Rebekah would have twin sons.
5. Later they would be two great nations.
6. Abraham, the boys' grandfather, lived uprightly and prayerfully.
7. Abraham died and God blessed Isaac richly.
8. Jacob and Esau, Isaac's sons, were quite different.
9. Jacob lived quietly in a tent and his farm was well cared for.
10. Once, Esau hunted until he was very hungry.
11. He looked longingly at the soup Jacob was making.
12. He foolishly sold his birthright for a bowl of soup.

B. Tell whether the underlined word is an adjective or an adverb. Remember: Adjectives tell which one? what kind? how many? Adverbs tell how? when? where? to what extent? (how much?) Use a stilum rubrum.

1. He looked <u>thoughtful</u>.
2. The girl gazed <u>thoughtfully</u> at the letter.
3. The price of the dress was very <u>high</u>.
4. Even a child can swing <u>high</u> on this swing!
5. <u>Soon</u> he will be flying.
6. She will be running <u>fast</u>.
7. The <u>fast</u> pitch landed in the catcher's mitt.
8. <u>Happily</u> they walked in the meadow.
9. They were <u>happy</u> to see the king.
10. <u>Now</u> they will live peaceably.

DAILY ORAL REVIEW

An adjective answers the questions *which one? what kind? how many?* about a noun.

An adjective agrees with the noun it modifies in gender, number, and case.

An adverb answers the questions *how? when? where? how much?* about a verb, an adjective, or another adverb.

Lesson Nine

Adverbs in Latin have the same use as in English. They modify verbs, adjectives, and other adverbs. Many times (but not always) Latin adverbs end in -$\bar{e}$.

To form an adverb from a first or second declension adjective, add -$\bar{e}$ to the adjective stem.

Adjective stem + $\bar{e}$ = adverb

ADJECTIVE		ADVERB	
altus	*high, deep*	altē	*on high, deeply*
longus	*long*	longē	*far off, by far*
miser	*sad, wretched*	miserē	*sadly, wretchedly*
pulcher	*beautiful*	pulchrē	*beautifully*

Lesson Nine Exercises

A. Study these new vocabulary words.

cantō, -āre, -āvī, -ātum

deus, -ī, m.

lātus, -a, -um

palla, -ae, f.

vir, virī, m

cicāda, -ae, f.	grasshopper
inter (*acc.*)	between, among
iūcundus, -a, -um	pleasant
lacerta, -ae, f.	lizard
mactō, -āre, -āvī, -ātum	to offer up, to slay, to sacrifice
monumentum, -ī, n.	monument
nōn iam	no longer
ōlim	one day, once upon a time
ruīna, -ae, f.	ruin
templum, -ī, n.	temple
toga, -ae, f.	toga, the robe of a Roman man
undique	on every side, from all sides
victima, -ae, f.	victim

B. Read the story. The adverbs are underlined for you.

ROMA

<u>Olim</u> Rōmānī parvum oppidum habitābant. <u>Nunc</u> magna et splendida est Rōma; magnae et lātae sunt viae oppidī. In angulīs viārum rosae sunt; Rōmānī templīs et monumentīs viās ornant. <u>Olim</u> in Forō Rōmānō templa multa et splendida erant. <u>Cotīdiē</u> virī Rōmānī in Forō ambulābant. Albae erant togae virōrum, sed rubrae et caeruleae et croceae erant pallae fēminārum. Arae <u>quoque</u> in Forō erant. In ārīs Rōmānī multās victimās deīs Rōmānīs mactābant. <u>Nōn iam</u> templa sunt in Forō Rōmānō. Nōn iam mactant Rōmānī victimās in ārīs. Sed <u>etiam</u> <u>nunc</u> pulchrum est Forum Rōmānum. Multae sunt ruinae; multae rosae inter ruinās sunt. Inter ruinās et rosās parvae lacertae properant. Pulchrae et iūcundae sunt lacertae. Cicādae <u>quoque</u> <u>undique</u> cantant. Lacertīs et cicādīs grātum est caelum caeruleum.

Vocabulary:

Rōma, -ae, f.—Rome   *Rōmānus, -ī,* m.—a Roman

C. Write an original sentence using the adverb given.

1. placidē _____

_____

2. iūcundē _____

_____

3. lātē _____

_____

4. pulchrē _____

_____

5. sōlum _____

_____

D. Give ten English derivatives from this lesson's vocabulary.

1. _____
2. _____
3. _____
4. _____
5. _____
6. _____
7. _____
8. _____
9. _____
10. _____

Lesson Ten

We have learned that adjectives modify nouns or pronouns, and we have learned to use many adjectives in our writing. Possessive pronouns are a special group of adjectives. They are used to show ownership. In English the possessive pronouns are: *my, mine, your, yours, his, her, hers, its, our, ours, their, theirs.* Study the personal pronouns in these sentences. Notice that they modify a noun, like an adjective does. They answer the adjective question *which one?*

> *Joshua told the people that Canaan was* their *land.*
> *Joshua prepared* his *army for battle.*
> *Rahab hid spies on* her *roof.*
> *When Jericho was destroyed, Rahab and* her *family were safe.*
> *"Our God is great," Joshua told* his *people.*
> *"Prepare* your *hearts to worship."*

In Latin, the possessive pronouns are often omitted when the meaning is clear without them. When they are used, however, they agree with the nouns they modify in gender, number, and case. They look like adjectives.

Here is a chart of the possessive pronouns.

IF THE NOUN BELONGS TO ONE PERSON

1st Person	meus, mea, meum, (*my*)
2nd Person	tuus, tua, tuum, (*your*)
3rd Person	suus, sua, suum, (reflexive . . . *his own*)

IF A NOUN BELONGS TO MORE THAN ONE PERSON

1st Person	noster, nostra, nostrum, (*our*)
2nd Person	vester, vestra, vestrum, (*your*)
3rd Person	suus, sua, suum (reflexive . . . *their own*)

Like any other adjective, a possessive pronoun agrees with the noun it modifies in gender, number, and case. The gender of the owner is not important. Study these examples of possessive pronouns.

Ad patriam nostram *nāvigābimus.*

Cerēs cum fīliā suā *habitābat.*

Patruus meus *fīliam* tuam *ad patriam* suam *portat.*

Ubi est fīlia mea?

Lesson Ten Exercises

A. Decline each of the possessive pronouns we studied in this chapter.

B. Write ten sentences of your own using possessive pronouns and vocabulary from lessons seven and nine.

1. _____

2. _____

3. _____

4. _____

5. _____

6. _____

7. _____

8. _____

9. _____

10. _____

C. Give an English derivative for each Latin verb.

1. dormītō (to sleep)   _____

2. habeō (to have)   _____

3. lacrimō (to cry)   _____

4. maneō (to stay)   _____

5. sedeō (to sit)   _____

Lesson Eleven

Being able to write and speak sentences is very important, but sometimes when we communicate we need to ask questions. In Latin there are several ways to ask questions.

We may place the verb at the beginning of a sentence and add *-ne* to it.

Eratne agricola in agrō?

Portantne plaustrī multās ūvās?

Nārratne famula parvae puellae fābulam?

Sometimes *minimē* (not at all) and *ita* (yes, thus) are used to answer questions instead of a complete sentence.

We may also form questions by using adverbs like *ubi* (where, where from?), *cūr* (why?), *unde* (where to?), and *quandō* (when?)

Cūr Britannī equīs arābant?

Quandō cēna in mensā erit?

Ubi sum?

Unde ambulābimus?

Lesson Eleven Exercises

A. Ask these questions in Latin. Be courageous! Break the sentence into small parts and work on one part at a time. Find the question word; find the verb; find the subject; find the direct object; find the prepositional phrases. *You can do it!*

1. Why is the sailor walking into the splendid town?

_____

2. Where is his small boat?

_____

3. Is he looking at your beautiful daughter in the field?

_____

4. Will the wicked pirate carry many red helmets in his ship?

_____

_____

5. Will the frightened townspeople hurry from the town in vain?

_____

_____

6. From where does the kind and fearless farmer walk?

_____

_____

7. When were the pirates hurrying away from the town?

_____

8. Why are the happy townspeople singing and dancing?

_____

9. Will the sailor and your daughter praise the strong farmer?

_____

_____

10. Were we singing from all sides?

_____

DAILY ORAL REVIEW

Decline *puella bona*, *puer bonus*, *dōnum bonum*.

Conjugate *vocō* in the present, imperfect, and future tenses.

Conjugate *sum* in the present, imperfect, and future tenses.

Lesson Twelve

We have learned three verb tenses, present, perfect, and future. These are sometimes called the present system because in Latin they add tense signs and personal endings to the present stem.

There are three other verb tenses. These are called the perfect tenses because in Latin they add tense signs and personal endings to the perfect stem.

We have been using the imperfect tense to tell of continuing action in the past. The action was not completed all at once.

Now we will learn about the *perfect tense*, the verb tense which tells about a past action which was done only once or was completed in a short period of time.

```
 \    All Past Times     \ Present /      Future Times      /
 Perfect   Imperfect    Present           Future
 < —.——~~~~—]----------[————————————>
```

In English, this verb tense is expressed by using the past form of the verb (usually identified by the *-ed* ending), or by using *has* or *have* or *did* with the past form of the verb. When *have* or *has* or *did* is used with another verb, it is called a "helping verb" and is counted as part of the verb.

These sentences express completed past action using the perfect tense.

Joseph's family *moved* to Goshen.

Pharoah *has enslaved* Joseph's family.

A princess *adopted* Moses.

The Hebrews *did escape* from Egypt.

Many English verbs have irregular past forms. These verbs do not add *-ed* to show perfect tense action. Because we use these words every day, we do not think of them as *irregular*. Read these sentences which also express the perfect tense.

He *ran* to the store and home again.

He *has run* to the store.

She *took* seven puppies to the farm.

She *has taken* seven rabbits, too.

Last week, I *saw* a robin.

We *have seen* ten squirrels at one time!

Lesson Twelve Exercise

A. Underline the perfect verbs. Use a stilum fuscum!

1. God gave His people rules for living.

2. The people promised to obey the rules.

3. Moses broke the stone tablet because the people were worshiping a gold calf while he was talking with God.

4. Later, they did follow God's instructions and built a special place to worship Him.

5. God promised His protection for the people as they were traveling in the wilderness.

6. The leaders counted the people before they left Mt. Sinai.

7. The families lined up for the march.

8. Before leaving, each family celebrated the Passover Feast.

9. The people were complaining about having no meat, so God gave them meat and a punishment.

10. Spies reported that Canaan was a good land.

B. Underline the perfect verbs, cross out the imperfect verbs.
Do not mark verbs which are not imperfect or perfect forms.

1. The people complained all the time.

2. Twelve spies scouted in Canaan.

3. Joshua and Caleb said the people should move to this good land.

4. The other ten men, who were not trusting God, were saying that the Canaanites were too tall for the Hebrews to overcome.

5. The earth did swallow one group of disobedient Hebrews.

6. Moses hit a rock instead of speaking to it.

7. Aaron died in the wilderness.

8. The people wandered around and around for forty years.

9. Once, God punished them by sending snakes into camp.

10. Moses prayed and God told him to make a bronze snake on a pole for the people to look at and be healed.

Lesson Thirteen

In Latin the *perfect tense* is formed by finding the perfect stem of the verb and adding the perfect tense personal endings. This is a special set of endings used only for this tense. To find the perfect stem, think of the third principal part of the verb and take off the *-ī*.

Perfect stem = third principal part - *ī*

Perfect tense = perfect stem + perfect personal endings

For the verb *vocō*, we see the listing: *vocō, -āre, -āvī, -ātum*. The third principle part is *vocāvī*. Take off the *-ī*, and the perfect stem is *vocāv-*. To this stem we add the perfect personal endings: *-ī, -istī, -it, -imus, -istis, -ērunt*.

This paradigm is for perfect verbs of the first conjugation.

PERFECT

vocā*vī*	I called	vocā*vimus*	we called
vocā*vistī*	you called	vocā*vistis*	you (pl.) called
vocā*vit*	he, she, it called	vocā*vērunt*	they called

The perfect tense for *sum* looks like this:

PERFECT

fu*ī*	I was, I have been	fu*imus*	we have been
fu*istī*	you have been	fu*istis*	you (pl.) have been
fu*it*	he, she, it has been	fu*ērunt*	they have been

Lesson Thirteen Exercises

A. Write the noun paradigm for these noun phrases.

toga

_____   _____

_____   _____

_____   _____

_____   _____

_____   _____

vir iūcundus

_____   _____

_____   _____

_____   _____

_____   _____

_____   _____

magnum templum

_____   _____

_____   _____

_____   _____

_____   _____

B. Conjugate these verbs orally in the perfect tense.

arō

cantō

nōminō

pugnō

saltō

C. Use each of the verbs in a sentence telling about a single completed past action.

1. arō   _____

2. cantō   _____

3. nōminō   _____

4. pugnō   _____

5. saltō   _____

D. Study these new vocabulary words.

cūrō, -āre, -āvī, -ātum

dēlectō, -āre, -āvī, -ātum

ōrō, -āre, -āvī, -ātum

capillus, -ī, m

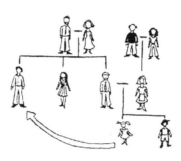

patruus, -ī, m.

adōrō, -āre, -āvī, -ātum	to worship
frūmentum, -ī, n.	grain, corn
herbōsus, -a, -um	grassy
incitō, -āre, -āvī, -ātum	to incite, to urge on
locus, -ī, m.	place (loca, plural neuter)
prātum, -ī, n.	meadow
prōcūl *(adv.)*	far, far away
statim *(adv.)*	at once
subitō *(adv.)*	suddenly
ūnus, -a, -um	one
vehementer *(adv.)*	exceedingly, very much

E. Give ten English derivatives from this lesson's vocabulary.

1. _____   6. _____

2. _____   7. _____

3. _____   8. _____

4. _____   9. _____

5. _____   10. _____

F. Read the story. Think about the difference in meaning between the imperfect tense and the perfect tense verbs.

CERĒS ET PERSEPHONĒ (A)

Nunc ūnum Deum adōrant et Italī et Britannī. Sed ōlim Rōmānī multōs deōs, multās deās, adōrābant. Dē deīs Rōmānīs fābulās nārrābō. Cerēs erat dea frūmentā; in agrīs frūmentum, in prātīs herbam cūrābat. Flāvum est frūmentum; flāvī erant deae capillī. Caerulea erat deae palla. Persephonē erat fīliā deae. Cerēs fīliam cāram vēhementer amābat. In īnsulā Siciliā Cerēs cum fīliā habitābat. Olim Persephonē in prātīs errābat. Cum puellā aliae puellae errābant, nam locus herbōsus fuit grātus puellīs laetīs. In prātō herbōsō puellae saltābant et cantābant. Multae rosae, multa līlia, in prātīs erant. Līlia alba puellās dēlectābant. Sed Plūtō, patruus puellae, deae fīliam procul spectāvit. Statim puellam vēhementer amāvit. Subitō equōs caeruleōs incitāvit et per prātam properāvit, et puellam perterritam raptāvit. Tum Persephonē, "O Cerēs," exclāmat, "ubi es? Patruus meus fīliam tuam ad Inferōs portat."

Vocabulary:

alius, -a, -ud—another

Cerēs, Cereris, f.—Ceres, goddess of grain

Inferī, -ōrum, m. pl.—The Underworld, the realm of the dead

līlium -ī, n.—lily

Persephonē, -ēs, f.—Persephone, daughter of Ceres

Plūtō, -ōnis, m.—Pluto, king of the Underworld

Sicilia, -ae, f.—Sicily

G. Answer these questions about the story with complete Latin sentences.

1. Quis (who) erat dea frūmentī?
2. Ubi Cerēs habitābat?
3. Ubi laetae Persephonē et puellae fuērunt?
4. Ubi līlia erant?
5. Cūr (why) Plūtō puellam raptāvit?

Lesson Fourteen

Conjunctions are small words which join together sentences, clauses, phrases, or words. The word *conjunction* comes from two Latin words, *com* (from *cum*, with) and *jungere* (to join).

Here is a list of frequently used Latin conjunctions.

atque—and, and also

aut—or

aut . . . aut—either . . . or

autem—but, however

et—and

et . . . et—both . . . and

itaque—and so

sed—but

quod—because

nam—for

nec—and not, nor

nec . . . nec—neither . . . nor

neque—and not, nor

neque . . . neque—neither . . . nor

An excellent way to learn to use these words well is by writing long sentences using conjunctions!

Lesson Fourteen Exercises

A. Study this new vocabulary.

cibus, -ī, m.

lūna, -ae, f.

īrātus, -a, -um

pōmum, -ī, n.

miser, -era, -erum   unhappy, unfortunate, poor
nusquam *(adv.)*   nowhere
passus, -a, -um   spread out, dishevelled

B. Read the story. Draw a cartoon strip (or three or four pictures in a row) showing what is happening in the story.

CERĒS ET PERSEPHONĒ (B)

Cerēs nōn in Siciliā erat, sed iam ad īnsulam properāvit. Nusquam erat Persephonē. Tum dea, īrāta et perterrita, passīs capillīs per terrās errābat. Per clīvōs altōs, per campōs lātōs, per silvās et agrōs, per terrās et caelum fīliam vocābat. Frustrā agricolās, frustrā lūnam et stellās rōgābat: "Ubi est fīlia mea?" Sed neque agricolae neque lūna neque stellae deae puellam monstrāvērunt. Nōn iam deae miserae grātum erat frūmentum; nōn iam herba erat in prātīs, neque ūvae purpureae in vīneās, neque pōma in agrōs, quod dea īrāta neque herbam neque vīneās neque pōma cūrābat. Frustrā iuvēncī albī agrōs arābant. Nōn iam cibum in plaustrīs magnīs ad oppida portābant.

Lesson Fifteen

The *pluperfect tense* is sometimes called the past perfect tense. *Pluperfect* comes from two Latin words *plus* and *perfect*, and it means "more than perfect." A pluperfect action was completed before another past action. We use the helping verb *had* with this tense.

> *Before his death, Joshua* had commanded *the Israelites well.*

> *But the people* had not destroyed *their enemies before they stopped to rest.*

> *God* had made *their lives hard so they would remember Him.*

> *When they* had prayed *for help, God sent them judges.*

> *Barak* had been afraid *to go into battle before Deborah, the woman judge, agreed to go with him.*

On a timeline, the pluperfect would look like this:

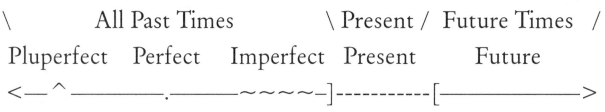

\   All Past Times   \ Present / Future Times /

Pluperfect   Perfect   Imperfect Present   Future

<—^————.————~~~~-]----------[————>

To form a pluperfect tense verb in Latin, we find the verb's perfect stem (the third principal part). Then we add the tense sign (*erā*) and the personal endings (*-m, -s, -t, -mus, -tis, -nt*).

> ## Pluperfect tense = perfect stem + *erā* + personal endings

This is the paradigm for pluperfect, first conjugation verbs.

PLUPERFECT

vocāv*eram*	I had called	vocāv*erāmus*	we had called
vocāv*erās*	you had called	vocāv*erātis*	you (pl.) had called
vocāv*erat*	he, she, it had called	vocāv*erant*	they had called

The pluperfect paradigm for *sum* looks like this:

PLUPERFECT

fu*eram*	I had been	fu*erāmus*	we had been
fu*erās*	you had been	fu*erātis*	you (pl.) had been
fu*erat*	he, she, it had been	fu*erant*	they had been

Lesson Fifteen Excercises

A. Tell (or write) the tense of the verbs in these English sentences. Choose from present(P), imperfect(I), future(F), perfect(PF), and pluperfect(PP).

_____1. Esau was the favored son of his father, Isaac.

_____2. Rebekah had made Jacob her favorite.

_____3. Perhaps Esau's choice of Canaanite wives made Rebekah grieved (*adj.*) with him.

_____4. Esau did not care that God had cursed the Canaanites.

_____5. Still Isaac loves his wayward son.

_____6. Isaac was planning to give Esau the blessing of the firstborn.

_____7. But Rebekah planned with Jacob to trick Isaac.

_____8. Jacob killed two goats which his mother fixed to taste like venison.

_____9. After Isaac had blessed Jacob, Esau appeared with his meal for his father.

_____10. Esau was searching for Jacob, but Jacob had gone to his Uncle's land.

B. Study this new vocabulary.

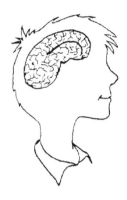

animus, -ī, m.

auxilium, auxiliī, n.

ēvolō, -āre, -āvī -ātum

familia, -ae, f.

populus, -ī, m.

ventus, -ī, m.

apportō, -āre, -āvī, -ātum	to bring, to take
celeriter *(adv.)*	quickly
dictum, -ī, n	a saying
factum, -ī, n.	deed, act
intereā *(adv.)*	meanwhile
lectus, -ī, m.	bed, couch
māne *(adv.)*	in the morning
memoria, -ae, f.	memory
mox *(adv.)*	soon
propter *(prep. w/ acc.)*	on account of, because of
semper *(adv.)*	always

C. Conjugate *apportō* and *ēvolō* in the perfect and pluperfect tenses. Conjugate *sum* in all five tenses.

PERFECT

apportāvī

_____   _____

_____   _____

PLUPERFECT

_____   _____

_____   _____

_____   _____

PERFECT

      ēvolāvī

_____   _____

_____   _____

PLUPERFECT

_____   _____

_____   _____

_____   _____

PRESENT

      sum

_____   _____

_____   _____

IMPERFECT

_____   _____

_____   _____

_____   _____

FUTURE

_____   _____

_____   _____

_____   _____

PERFECT

_____   _____

_____   _____

_____   _____

PLUPERFECT

_____   _____

_____   _____

_____   _____

D. Read the story of Jacob and Esau in Genesis 27. Next read this short version of the story. Notice the use of different tenses. Then draw a picture on the next page to show your understanding of the part of the story written here.

Isaac oculīs nōn spectāverat, vocāvitque Esau fīlium suum maiorem et "Fīlī mī," inquit. Esau respondit, "Adsum."

"Tibi ōrō, bēstiam armīs tuīs necā et mihi cēnam creā," dixit Isaac. Ita Esau in silvā et in agrīs ambulābat.

Intereā Rebekah fīliō suō Jacob narrāverat, "Necā duās parvās bēstiās, dabimus cibum Isaac." Tum Rebekah togam Esau portāverat et Jacob togam cum multīs capillīs creāverat. Posteā Jacob ad Isaac cibum portāvit. Isaac putāvit Jacob Esau esse. Tum Isaac Jacob magnum benedictum dedit.

Mox Esau cibum suum portāvit ad Isaac. "Nōn es Esau," dixit Isaac, "Māne Esau erat hic. Esau benedictum dedī." Lacrimīs sed frustrā, Esau ōrāvit, "Dā mihi benedictum." Tum Isaac Esau parvum benedictum dedit. Nunc Esau īrātus erat propter Jacob. Familia maesta erat quod Jacob et Rebekah stultī et scelerātī fuerant.

Vocabulary:
maiorem—older
filī mī—my son
adsum, adesse, adfuī—to be present
tibi—to you
creō, -āre, -āvī, -ātum—create, make
necā—Kill! a command
putō, -āre, -āvī, -ātum—to think

posteā—afterwards
dixit—he said
hic (adv.)—here
dā—Give!
stultus, -a, -um—foolish
scelerātus, -a, -um—wicked

Lesson Sixteen

The last verb tense we have to learn is the *future perfect* tense. This tense is hardly ever seen in English; it's meaning is understood, not directly stated. In Latin, also, this tense does not often appear, but learning it will complete our ability to conjugate a verb and prepare us for those times it is used.

The future perfect tense tells one future action which happens before another future action. (The second future action will be in the future tense.) The helping verbs for this tense are *will have*.

Here are some examples of future perfect tense verbs in English sentences.

When you will have plowed *the field, we will plant it.*

Before he will have jumped *his final hurdle he* will have run *ten miles.*

After he will have finished *his ice cream, he will go to bed.*

On a timeline, the future perfect would look like this:

```
\        All Past Times          \ Present /        Future Times              /
Pluperfect  Perfect    Imperfect   Present    Future Perfect    Future
  <—^————————.————~~~~—]————————[———————*————————————————>
```

To form a future perfect tense verb in Latin, we find the verb's perfect stem (the third principal part). Then we add the tense sign (*eri*) and the personal endings (*-ō, -s, -t, -mus, -tis, -nt*).

Future Perfect tense = perfect stem + *eri* + personal endings.

This is the paradigm for future perfect, first conjugation verbs:

FUTURE PERFECT

vocāver*ō*	I will have called	vocāver*imus*	we will have called
vocāver*is*	you will have called	vocāver*itis*	you (pl.) will have called
vocāver*it*	he, she, it will have called	vocāver*int*	they will have called

The future perfect paradigm for *sum* looks like this:

FUTURE PERFECT

fuer*ō*	I will have been	fuer*imus*	we will have been
fuer*is*	you will have been	fuer*itis*	you (pl.) will have been
fuer*it*	he, she, it will have been	fuer*int*	they will have been

Lesson Sixteen Exercises

A. Study these vocabulary words.

aeger, aegra, aegrum

gelidus, -a, -um

osculum, -ī, n.

saxum, -ī, n.

adhūc *(adv.)*	still, yet
cūnae, -ārum, f.	cradle
diū *(adv.)*	for a long time
dīvīnus, -a, -um	divine
ē, ex *(prep. w/ abl.)*	out of, from
ecce	behold
gremium, -ī, n.	lap
ibi *(adv.)*	there
ignōtus, -a, -um	unknown
maestus, -a, -um	sad
mīrus, -a, -um	wonderful
plēnus, -a, -um	full
post *(prep. w/ acc.)*	after
rusticus, -a, -um	rustic, belonging to the country
tamen *(adv.)*	however, still, nevertheless
tandem *(adv.)*	at last
tōtus, -a, -um	whole

B. Use each of this lesson's adjectives in a Latin sentence with a future perfect verb.

1. aeger _____

2. dīvīnus _____

3. gelidus _____

4. ignōtus _____

5. maestus _____

6. mīrus _____

7. plēnus _____

8. rusticus _____

9. tōtus _____

10. purpureus _____

C. Tell why?

1. Why does the word for cradle only have plural forms?

2. Why is an *osculation* not something proper to do in public? (or at least not usually!)

3. Why does a plant family have the name *saxifrage*?

4. Why is an *exit* a place for going out?

5. Why is a feeling of *plenitude* a good thing?

Daily Oral Review

Conjugate a different verb each day. Use all six tenses.

Decline an adjective/noun phrase each day.

Review the definitions of the parts of speech.

Lesson Seventeen

A way to look quickly at all the tenses of a verb is called a *synopsis*. To do a synopsis of any verb, we simply follow the same personal pronoun through all the tenses. In English we would do a synopsis of *talk* in the first person, singular, by saying: *I talk, I was talking, I shall talk, I have talked, I had talked, I shall have talked.* To keep from being confused, we always use the same order for a conjugation or a synopsis. We follow the order in which we learned the tenses: present, imperfect, future, perfect, pluperfect, future perfect.

A synopsis of *vocō* in the third person, singular looks like this:

PRESENT	voca*t*
IMPERFECT	vocā*bat*
FUTURE	vocā*bit*
PERFECT	vocā*vit*
PLUPERFECT	vocā*verat*
FUTURE PERFECT	vocā*verit*

Lesson Seventeen Exercises

A. Do a synopsis of these verbs as required.

CANTŌ: FIRST PERSON, SINGULAR

Present _____

Imperfect _____

Future _____

Perfect _____

PluPerfect _____

Future Perfect _____

ARŌ: SECOND PERSON, PLURAL

_____

_____

_____

_____

_____

EXCLĀMŌ: FIRST PERSON, PLURAL

_____

_____

_____

_____

_____

Lesson Eighteen

There are four family groups, or conjugations, of Latin verbs. The first conjugation has an infinitive ending in *-āre*. The second group has an infinitive ending in *-ēre*. Many of the tenses will look almost like first conjugation tenses, but they will have an *-ē-* in the present stem. These verbs will be listed in a vocabulary or dictionary listing as: *sedeō, -ēre, sēdī, sessum*. Each verb will have its very own third and fourth principal part. They are not as easy to remember as the *-āre, -āvī, -ātum* pattern of first conjugation. It is important to memorize all four parts when you first learn the vocabulary.

The second conjugation paradigm for the present tense looks like this:

PRESENT

teneō	I hold, I am holding, I do hold	tenēmus	we hold
tenēs	you hold	tenētis	you (pl.) hold
tenet	he, she, it holds	tenent	they hold

The second conjugation paradigm for the imperfect tense looks like this:

IMPERFECT

ten*ēbam*	I was holding	ten*ēbāmus*	we were holding
ten*ēbās*	you were holding	ten*ēbātis*	you (pl.) were holding
ten*ēbat*	he, she, it was holding	ten*ēbant*	they were holding

The second conjugation paradigm for the future tense looks like this:

FUTURE

ten*ēbō*	I shall hold	ten*ēbimus*	we shall hold
ten*ēbis*	you will hold	ten*ēbitis*	you (pl.) will hold
ten*ēbit*	he, she, it will hold	ten*ēbunt*	they will hold

Lesson Eighteen Exercises

A. Study these new vocabulary words.

habeō, habēre, habuī, habitum   iactō, iactāre, iactāvī, iactum

doceō, docēre, docuī, doctum	to teach
fleō, flēre, flēvī, flētum	to weep, to cry
flōreō, flōrēre, flōruī, — — —	to flourish, to flower
fulgeō, fulgēre, fulsī, — — —	to shine
iaceo, -ere, -cui, — — —	to lie
maneō, manēre, mānsī, mansum	to stay, to remain
sedeō, sedēre, sēdī, sessum	to sit
teneō, tenēre, tenuī, tentum	to hold
timeō, timēre, timuī, — — —	to fear, to be afraid
valeō, valēre, valuī, — — —	to be well
videō, vidēre, vīdī, vīsum	to see

B. Orally conjugate *habeō*, *sedeō*, and *videō* in the present, imperfect, and future tenses.

C. Make a list of at least ten English words which come from this lesson's vocabulary. Use a stilum nigrum.

D. Read the story. Circle each verb stilō flavō.

CERĒS ET PERSEPHONĒ (C)

Tandem Cerēs prope parvam casam agricolae in saxō gelidō sedēbat. Dea maesta diū lacrimābat. Tum ē casā parva puella ad deam vēnit. Puellae oculī plenī erant lacrimārum. "Parvum puerum," inquit, "habēmus. In cūnīs aeger iacet. Lacrimāmus, quod aeger est puer." Tum Cerēs lacrimās suās tenuit, et cum puellā ad casam properāvit.

Ibi Metanīra fīlium aegrum in gremiō tenēbat. Fīlius Metanīrae Triptolemus erat. Lacrimābant et agricola et Metanīra et parva puella, quod nōn valēbat puer. Tum Cerēs puerō osculum dedit, et ecce! statim valuit puer. Mīrum et dīvīnum erat osculum deae. Laetae erant et agricola et Metanīra et puella. Iam laetus et validus puer in cūnīs dormītābat. Tum Cerēs Triptolemum in gremiō suō tenuit. Dea cum tōtā familiā cēnam habuit; in mensā erant ūvae purpureae et pōma iūcunda. Adhūc ignōta erant Italīs Graecīsque et vīnum et frūmentum. Deae tamen flāvae grāta erat cēna rustica. Post cēnam in casā agricolae dea manēbat et cotidiē Triptolemum cūrābat.

Lesson Nineteen

In Latin the perfect tense for the second conjugation is formed by finding the perfect stem of the verb and adding the perfect tense personal endings. This is a special set of endings used only for this tense. To find the perfect stem, think of the third principal part of the verb and take off the *-ī*.

Perfect stem = third principal part *-ī*

Perfect tense =
perfect stem + perfect personal endings

For the verb *teneō*, we see the listing: *teneō, tenēre, tenuī, tentum*. The third principle part is *tenuī*. Take off the *-ī*, and the perfect stem is *tenu-*. To this stem we add the perfect personal endings: *-ī, -istī, -it, -imus, -istis, -ērunt*.

This is the paradigm for second conjugation perfect verbs.

PERFECT

tenu*ī*	I held, I have held	tenu*imus*	we held
tenu*istī*	you held	tenu*istis*	you (pl.) held
tenu*it*	he, she, it held	tenu*ērunt*	they held

The pluperfect and future perfect tenses follow the same rules as for first conjugation verbs.

This is the paradigm for pluperfect verbs of the second conjugation.

PluPerfect tense =
perfect stem + *erā* + personal endings

PLUPERFECT

tenu*eram*	I had held	tenu*erāmus*	we had held
tenu*erās*	you had held	tenu*erātis*	you (pl.) had held
tenu*erat*	he, she, it had held	tenu*erant*	they had held

Future Perfect tense = perfect stem + *eri* + personal endings

---

This is the paradigm for future perfect verbs of the second conjugation.

FUTURE PERFECT

tenu*erō*	I will have held	tenu*erimus*	we will have held
tenu*eris*	you will have held	tenu*eritis*	you (pl.) will have held
tenu*erit*	he, she, it will have held	tenu*erint*	they will have held

Lesson Nineteen Exercises

A. Review vocabulary from lessons 10–18.

B. Orally conjugate *portō* and *sedeō* in all six tenses.

C. Do a complete synopsis (all six tenses) of *maneō*, *iaceō*, and *doceō* in the third person plural.

MANEŌ:

Present _____

Imperfect _____

Future _____

Perfect _____

PluPerfect _____

Future Perfect _____

IACEŌ:

_____

_____

_____

_____

_____

_____

DOCEŌ:

_____

_____

_____

_____

_____

_____

D. How would you say this in Latin?

1. First, the temple had held the altars, then it held many rocks.

_____

2. Before I sleep, I will pray and praise God. (In Latin it will look like: Before I will sleep, I will have prayed and I will have praised God.)

_____

3. They were building cottages, but she wanted one wide palace.

_____

4. The forest and the red earth were beautiful on every side.

_____

5. The wicked woman's kind husband was sound asleep. (was lying in a deep sleep.)

_____

E. Read the story.

Iam lūna et stellae in caelō fulgēbant. Umbrae terrās et pontum profundum cēlābant. Per terrās virī et fēminae animōs somnō laxābant. Sed somnus Metanīram nōn tenēbat; furtim deam cum puerō spectābat.

Cerēs prope puerī cūnās stābat. Vērba mīra et dīvīna cantābat. Tum puerum in gremiō tenuit, et ad focum ambulāvit. Ecce! Triptolemus in focō inter flammās iacēbat sed laetus erat puer; neque focum neque flammās timuit. Sed Metanīra, perterrita, "O fīlī mī," exclāmāvit, et ad focum properāvit.

Tum dea īrāta puerum ē flammās raptāvit et humī iactāvit, et Metanīrae, "O fēmina," inquit, " stulta et scelerāta fuistī. Nōn deus erit Triptolemus, quod stultae fēminae est fīlius. Sed in gremiō deae iacuit; itaque magnus vir erit. Et ego et Persephonē, fīlia mea, Triptolemum docēbimus et cūrābimus. Agricolārum magister erit, nam frūmentum et vīnum agricolīs monstrābit."

Vocabulary:

axō, -āre, -āvī, -ātum—to relax, to loosen	*pontus, -ī, m.*—sea
focus, -ī, m.—hearth	*somnus, -ī m.*—sleep
furtim (adv.)—secretly, stealthily	*verbum, -ī, n.*—word

F. Answer these questions about the grammatical constructions in the story.

1. What case is used for *pontum profundum*? Why?
2. What case is used for *virī (virī et fēminae)*? Why?
3. What case is used for *somnō*? Why?
4. What case is used for *focum (ad focum)*? Why?
5. Look at the sentence: *Verba mīra et dīvīna cantābat.* Why is the verb singular?
6. Make up your own question. Can you think of one your classmates can't answer?

Optional Unit—Stories

Tum Cerēs ē casā agricolae ambulāvit. Sed flēvērunt familia et flēvit Triptolemus, quod nōn iam in gremiō deae dormītābat. Māne agricola virōs et fēminās locī convocāvit, et dicta deae et facta narrāvit. Deinde virī et fēminae multa saxa apportāvērunt et magnum templum aedificāvērunt. In templī ārīs victimās mactāvērunt, et deam adōrāvērunt. Grāta erant deae dōna populī, et Cerēs templum diū habitābat. Intereā in ārīs aliōrum deōrum neque pōma neque ūvae neque rosae iacēbant. Nōn iam herba in prātīs, nōn iam pōma in agrīs flōrēbant, quod adhūc Cerēs propter fīliam flēbat. Itaque Iuppiter deae, "Plūto," inquit, "fīliam tuam habet. Persephonē rēgīna Inferōrum est. Sed Mecurius ad regnum Inferōrum properābit, et puellam ad templum tuum celeriter apportābit." Deinde Mercurius ad Inferōs properāvit. Persephonē cum virō suō in lectō sedēbat. Misera erat puella, quod adhūc deam cāram dēsīderābat. Sed Mercurium vidēbat et laeta fuit. "Iterum," inquit, "deam cāram vidēbo, iterum Cerēs fīliam suam habēbit." Tum Plūto vērbīs benignīs puellam ōrāvit : "O Persephonē, memoriae tuae grātus semper erit Plūto; iterum rēgīna Inferōrum eris. Nunc caeruleum est caelum, iūcunda sunt prāta, sed mox gelidum erit caelum, gelidī erunt et vēntī et agrī. Tum iterum virum tuum et regnum Inferōrum dēsīderābis. Valē, O cāra rēgīna." Tum Persephonē cum Mercuriō ē regnō Inferōrum properāvit. Mercurius equōs validōs incitāvit, et equī per clīvōs altōs, per campōs lātōs libenter properāvērunt. Tandem Persephonē templum deae flāvae vidēbat. Puella laeta verbīs laetīs deam vocāvit. Cerēs magnō gaudiō ē templō ēvolāvit, et fīliae cārae multa oscula dabat. Subitō per terrās herba in prātīs, ūvae in vīneīs undique flōrēbant, quod nōn iam flēbant Cerēs et Persephonē. Cēterī quoque deī laetī erant, quod agricolae ad templa multa dōna apportābant et in ārīs victimās mactābant.

Vocabulary:

deinde (adv.)—then, next

Iuppiter, Iovis, m.—Jupiter, king of the gods

Mercurius, -ī, m.—Mercury, messenger of the gods

gaudium, -ī, n.—joy

regnum, -ī, n.—kingdom

valē, valēte (pl.)—goodbye (be well)

cēterī, -ae, -a—the rest

libenter (adv.)—willingly, gladly

Lesson Twenty

We learned that there are five declensions for Latin nouns. In this text we will learn the third declension, which is a large noun family. The fourth and fifth declensions we will study in a later text.

The third declension has nouns that are masculine, feminine, or neuter in gender. All third declension nouns have a genitive form

> First declension genitive ends in *-ae*.
> Second declension genitive ends in *-ī*
> Third declension genitive ends in *-is*.

ending in *-is*. The good habits we've begun by learning the gender with the vocabulary word will be even more useful now. It is also important in this declension to memorize each genitive form so that we have the correct stem on which to add the case endings.

Masculine and feminine nouns of the third declension have the same paradigm. The neuter paradigm is a bit different because it follows the neuter noun rule. (The nominative and accusative cases look alike, and the nominative and accusative plurals end in -*a*.)

This is the paradigm for *masculine* and *feminine* third declension nouns.

CASE	SINGULAR	PLURAL
Nominative	mīles	mīlitēs
Genitive	mīlitis	mīlitum
Dative	mīlitī	mīlitibus
Accusative	mīlitem	mīlitēs
Ablative	mīlite	mīlitibus

This is the paradigm for *neuter* third declension nouns.

CASE	SINGULAR	PLURAL
Nominative	caput	capita
Genitive	capitis	capitum
Dative	capitī	capitibus
Accusative	caput	capita
Ablative	capite	capitibus

Most of the words for members of the family (father, mother, aunt, uncle, brother, sister, etc.) come from third declension nouns. Many words for parts of the body and the words for plants and animals also come from third declension nouns.

Here are some hints for remembering the genitive and the gender of third declension nouns:

Nouns of one syllable ending in -*x* are mostly feminine.

Nouns of one syllable ending in *consonant* + -*s* are *feminine*. (except *fōns, mōns, pōns,* and *dēns,* which are *masculine*)

English derivatives sometimes give clues about the genitive form: *dental* (dēns, *denti*s, m. tooth) *legal* (lēx, *lēgi*s, f. law).

The exercises for this lesson will contain many new vocabulary words from these three groups. Study each group of words until you are comfortable with it. Then move on to the next exercise.

Lesson Twenty Exercises

A. Study the vocabulary for family members. Notice that not all the words are from the third declension.

FAMILY TREE

avia, -ae, f. – grandmother

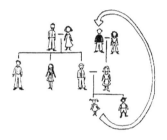

avus, -ī, m. – grandfather

pater, patris, m. – father

māter, matris, f.– mother

frāter, fratris, m. – brother

soror, sorōris, f. – sister

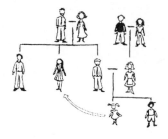

amita, -ae, f. – aunt

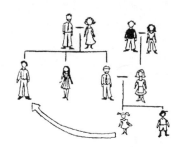

patruus, -ī, m. – uncle

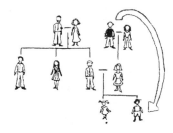

nepos, nepōtis, m. – grandson

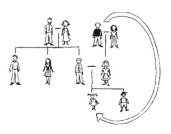

neptis, neptis*, f. – granddaughter

uxor, -ōris, f. – wife

*I-stem noun, Lesson 21

līberī, -ōrum, m. pl.	children
sōbrīna, -ae, f.	cousin (only on the mother's side)
sōbrīnus -ī, m.	cousin
	[To speak of a cousin on the father's side, one must use the third declension adjective (in a future lesson!) patruēlis, -e]
virgō, -inis, f.	virgin, young woman

B. Practice the third declension masculine/feminine paradigm using pater, māter, frāter, soror. Then write the paradigms for *pater bonus* and *māter bona*! Remember: an adjective agrees with the noun it modifies in gender, number, and case.

pater bonus _____

_____   _____

_____   _____

_____   _____

_____   _____

māter bona _____

_____   _____

_____   _____

_____   _____

C. From the vocabulary in this lesson, tell how we may have derived these English words and phrases.

Fraternal Order of Police

maternal instincts

paternalistic

nepotism

sorority

virgin

uxorious

D. Write a Latin composition about your family. Be sure to use descriptive adjectives for each person.

E. Study the parts of the body. Take turns with your classmates inventing sentences for a story about a very sick man. Be sure to have your adjectives agreeing with the nouns they modify in gender, number, and case.

caput, capitis, n. – head

cor, cordis, n. – heart

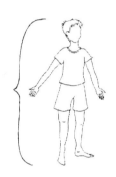

corpus, corporis, n. – body

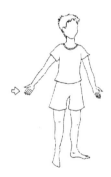

dextra, -ae, f. – right hand

bracchium, -ī, n. – arm

collum, -ī, n. – neck

genu, -ūs, n. (IV declension) – knee

pectus, -oris, n. – breast

pēs, pedis*, m. – foot

sinistra, -ae, f. – left hand

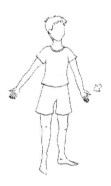

sinistrum, -ī, n. – left side

oculus, oculī, m. – eye

*I-stem noun, Lesson 21

Lesson Twenty-One

The third declension has a set of nouns which are called *I-stem* nouns. The paradigm for masculine and feminine I-stems differs from the regular third declension only in the genitive plural which ends in *-ium*. The neuter paradigm differs in four places (ablative singular, nominative and accusative plural, genitive plural).

To remember which third declension nouns are I-stems, follow these rules.

M/F I-stems:
1) nominative ends in *-es or -is* <u>and</u> genitive has same number of syllables as nominative
2) nominative singular ends in *-ns* or *-rs*
3) nominative singular is one syllable <u>and</u> stem ends in two consonants

---

> # Neuter I-stems:
> ## nominative singular ends in *-e, -al, -ar*

This is the paradigm for third declension *masculine* and *feminine* declension I-stem nouns.

CASE	SINGULAR	PLURAL
Nominative	nox	noct*ēs*
Genitive	noct*is*	noct*ium*
Dative	noct*ī*	noct*ibus*
Accusative	noct*em*	noct*ēs*
Ablative	noct*e*	noct*ibus*

This is the paradigm for third declension *neuter* I-stem nouns.

CASE	SINGULAR	PLURAL
Nominative	mar*e*	mar*ia*
Genitive	mar*is*	mar*ium*
Dative	mar*ī*	mar*ibus*
Accusative	mar*e*	mar*ia*
Ablative	mar*ī*	mar*ibus*

It may be helpful to mark the endings on the I-stem chart where they differ from regular third declension nouns.

Lesson Twenty-One Exercises

A. Study the vocabulary. The I-stem nouns are marked with an *.

īnfāns, īnfantis*, m/f	child
adolescens, -entis*, m/f	youth (*adj.*) young, youthful
iuvenis, -is*, m/f	young man or woman (*adj.*) young, youthful
parens, -entis*, m/f	parent
gēns, gentis*, f.	race
genus, -eris, n.	sort, kind, race
homō, hominis, m/f	man, human being
senex, senis, m/f	old person
mātrōna, -ae, f.	married woman, matron
mulier, -eris, f.	woman
marītus, -ī, m.	husband
mors, mortis*, f.	death

B. Solve the riddles. Who is

1. soror mātris?

2. frāter patris?

3. frāter patruī?

4. soror tuae?

5. māter mātris?

6. pater patris?

7. fīlia amitae?

8. fīlius patrī?

9. nōndum (not yet) ambulat?

10. nōn iam ambulat?

11. nōndum marītus, sed nōn infāns est?

12. nōn iam virgō et nōn adolescēns est?

C. Here is Psalm 148 as it appears in the Vulgate, the Latin translation of the Bible. Macrons have been added so that the words look more like what you are used to seeing. You will be able to read many parts of it. Look closely at verse 12.

1 Alleluia laudāte Dominum dē caelīs laudāte eum in excelsīs

2 laudāte eum omnēs angelī eius laudāte eum omnēs exercitus eius

3 laudāte eum sol et luna laudāte eum omnēs stellae luminis

4 laudāte eum caelī caelōrum et aquae quae super caelōs sunt

5 laudent nomen Dominī quoniam ipse mandāvit et creata sunt

6 et statuit ea in saeculum et in saeculum praeceptum dedit et nōn praeteribit

7 laudāte Dominum dē terrā draconēs et omnēs abyssī

8 ignis et grandō nix et glaciēs ventus turbō quae facitis sermonem eius

9 montēs et omnēs collēs lignum fructiferum et universae cedrī

10 bēstiae et omnia iumenta reptilia et avēs volantēs

11 regēs terrae et omnēs populī principēs et universī iudicēs terrae

12 iuvenēs et virginēs senēs cum puerīs laudent nomen Dominī

13 quoniam sublime nomen eius solius

14 gloria eius in caelō et in terrā et exaltāvit cornū populī suī laus omnibus sanctīs eius fīliīs Israhel populō adpropinquantī sibi Alleluia

Lesson Twenty-Two

The verb *possum* is an irregular verb in Latin. It is in the same family as *sum*, so it is very easy to learn it's conjugation. *Possum* means *I can,* or *I am able.* We get words like *omnipotent* (able to do all things) from *possum.*

Here is the paradigm of all six tenses of *possum, posse, potuī.*

PRESENT

possum	I can, I am able	possumus	we are able
potes	you are able	potestis	you (pl.) are able
potest	he, she, it is able	possunt	they are able

IMPERFECT

poteram	I was able, I could	poterāmus	we were able
poterās	you were able	poterātis	you (pl.) were able
poterat	he, she, it was able	poterant	they were able

FUTURE

poterō	I will be able	poterimus	we will be able
poteris	you will be able	poteritis	you (pl.) will be able
poterit	he, she, it will be able	poterunt	they will be able

PERFECT

potuī	I was, I have been able	potuimus	we have been able
potuistī	you have been able	potuistis	you (pl.) have been able
potuit	he, she, it has been able	potuērunt	they have been able

PLUPERFECT

potu*eram*	I had been able	potu*erāmus*	we had been able
potu*erās*	you had been able	potu*erātis*	you (pl.) had been able
potu*erat*	he, she, it had been able	potu*erant*	they had been able

FUTURE PERFECT

potu*erō*	I will have been able	potu*erimus*	we will have been able
potu*eris*	you will have been able	potu*eritis*	you will have been able
potu*erit*	he, she, it will have been able	potu*erint*	they will have been able

Lesson Twenty-Two Exercises

A. Many times the verb *possum* is used with an infinitive to convey the idea of *being able to do* something. Write good Latin sentences for these ideas.

1. I can call my brother from the fields.

_____

2. You were able to sail for three years. (Use ablative duration of time)

_____

3. She will be able to carry many rocks with a wagon.

_____

4. We have been able to teach the children many new words.

_____

5. You (pl.) had been able to see the moon and bright stars.

_____

6. They will have been able to hold the infants in (their) laps.

_____

7. The king's son was not able to give a gift to the daughter of the farmer. _____

_____

8. At last the husbands have been able to walk with their wives in the meadow. _____

_____

9. Children are able to flourish with kind, firm parents.

_____

10. Because of his deeds, his words have not been able to stay in their hearts _____

_____

DAILY ORAL REVIEW

Decline a noun from each declension.

fēmina

vir

verbum

mulier

caput

gēns

animal

Conjugate a verb from each conjugation. Add *sum* or *possum*.

spectō

fleō

Review adjective vocabulary.

Review adverb vocabulary.

Review prepositions.

Use each preposition in a phrase showing the case ending of the noun.

Optional Unit—Seasons and Weather

Now that we have learned the third declension, we will be able to say and write about many more things than we could before. Many of the words which relate to the world around us come from third declension nouns.

SPRING

vēr, vēris, n.	spring
primō vēre	in the beginning of spring
pluvia, -ae, f.	rain
imber, imbris, m.	shower or storm of rain
nimbus, -ī, m.	cloud
pluit, pluere, (plūvit)	it rains, it rained; to rain
procella, -ae, f.	storm, gale, wind squall
tempestās, tempestātis, f.	storm, tempest
arbor, arboris, f.	tree
flōs, flōris, m.	flower, blossom
folium, -ī, n.	leaf, foliage
rāmus, -ī, m.	bough, branch, twig
vireō, -ēre	to be green, to grow green or healthy
viridis, -e *(adj.)*	green

SUMMER

aestās, aestātis, f.	summer
aestāte novā	at the beginning of summer
sōl, sōlis, m.	sun

AUTUMN

autumnus, -ī, m.	autumn
autumnō vergente	towards the end of autumn

WINTER

hiems, hiemis, f.	winter
hieme	in winter
nix, nivis, f.	snow
niveus, -a, -um	snowy
nivātus, -a, -um	iced, cooled with snow
ningit, ningere, ninxit	it snows

Draw a picture of one of the seasons. (Or draw all of the seasons!) Label all the parts of your picture with a Latin word.

Lesson Twenty-Three

Much of our understanding of a language comes from understanding the people who speak the language. How people think, what they do, how they think about past deeds, all these things are part of a people's culture. Many times new words will develop to describe a new tool or action in a culture. For example, when your grandparents were children, the word *fax* was probably not in their dictionary. Now almost everyone knows what a fax machine is or how to send a fax.

In the story we will study in this lesson, we will learn how the meaning of the Latin verb *raptō* was forever set in history. From this word we get words like *rapid, rapture, rapine, rapt, raptor,* and *raptorial.*

In this story there are also many words which have to do with fighting or war. Look for the Latin words from which we get *armor, belligerent, clamor, fortitude, gladiator, military, pugnacious.*

Lesson Twenty-Three Exercises

A. Study the vocabulary.

eques, -itis, m. – horseman, knight; *pl.* – calvary

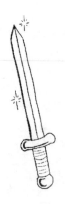

gladius, -ī, m. – sword

onus, -eris, n. – burden, load

rēx, rēgis, m. – king

scūtum, -ī, n. – shield

tempus, -oris, n. – time

arma, -ōrum, n. pl.	arms, weapons
armātus, -a, -um	armed
bellum, -ī, n.	war
cīvis, cīvis* m/f	citizen
cīvitās, -ātis, f.	state
citō *(adv.)*	quickly
fīnitimus, -a, -um	neighbouring
formōsus, -a, -um	beautiful, beautifully formed
medius, -a, -um	middle
mīles, mīlitis, m.	soldier
parō, -āre, -āvī, ātum	prepare
parvulus, -a, -um	very little, very small
pax, pācis, f.	peace
pedes, -itis, m.	foot soldier
urbs, urbis,* f.	city
vox, vōcis, f.	voice

B. Read the story.

ROMULUS ET SABINAE

Rōmulus erat fīlius Martis. Mars erat deus bellī et armōrum. Mīlitēs Rōmānī Martem adōrābant et in Martis ārīs victimās mactābant. Rōmulus igitur mīlitēs et arma vehementer amābat. Urbis Rōmae prīmus rēx erat. Sed sōlum virī urbem habitābant; neque uxōrēs neque sorōrēs habēbant.

Itaque Rōmulus tōtum populum convocāvit, et "O cīvēs," inquit, "nullās fēminās habēmus, sed Sabīnī cīvitātem fīnitimam habitant. Sabīnī fēminās multās et formōsās habent. Sabīnōs igitur cum fēminīs ad lūdōs invītābimus, et virginēs raptābimus."

Rōmānī igitur Sabīnōs ad lūdōs magnōs invītāvērunt. Pax erat inter Rōmānōs et Sabīnōs. Itaque Sabīnī ad lūdōs Rōmānōrum libenter properāvērunt. Nec scūta nec gladiōs nec hastās apportāvērunt. Cum Sabīnīs virginēs multae et formōsae properāvērunt. Sabīnī lūdōs Rōmānōrum spectāvērunt.

In mediīs lūdīs, Rōmānī magnā vōce subitō clāmāvērunt, et ecce! virginēs Sabīnās raptāvērunt et ad casās portāvērunt. Frustrā mātrēs lacrimāvērunt, frustrā virōs in arma incitāvērunt. Rōmānī scūta et gladiōs et hastās habēbant; Sabīnīs nec scūta nec gladiī nec hastae fuērunt.

Maestī igitur et īrātī Sabīnī ad terram Sabīnam properāvērunt. Per tōtam hiemem ibi manēbant et arma diligenter parābant. Via est longa inter Rōmam et terram Sabīnam. Sed tandem Sabīnī, iam armātī, ante portās urbis Rōmae stābant. "O Rōmānī," inquiunt, "prō fīliābus nostrīs, prō sorōribus nostrīs fortiter pugnābimus."

Deinde Sabīnae ē casīs Rōmānōrum passīs capillīs ēvolāvērunt; parvulōs portāvērunt et patribus frātribusque monstrāvērunt. Patrēs frātrēsque suōs multīs lacrimīs ōrāvērunt. "Nunc," inquiunt, "in casīs Rōmānīs laetae et placidae habitāmus; līberōs cārōs habēmus et vehementer

amāmus; et Sabīnōs et Rōminōs amāmus. Sī Rōmānī cum Sabīnīs
pugnābunt, Rōmānī Sabīnōs, Sabinī Rōmānōs necābunt. Tum Sabīnae
nec virōs nec patrēs nec frātrēs habēbunt. O patrēs, valēte! nōn iam
Sabīnae sed Rōmānae semper erimus fīliae vestrae."

Vocabulary:
Mars, Martis, m.—Mars, god of war
Rōmulus, -ī, m.—Romulus, the founder of Rome
Sabīnus, -ī, m.—a Sabine, a neighbor of the Romans
Sabīnus, -a, -um—Sabine, belonging to the Sabine tribe
Sabina, -ae, f.—a Sabine woman

C. From the Latin words in the story and how they are used, write your own definitions for the following English words.

evolution _____

filial _____

adore _____

urban _____

habitation _____

civil _____

invitation _____

ludicrous _____

multitude _____

null _____

D. Imagine that you were a Sabine boy or girl at the games. Write a story in Latin from your viewpoint. Use many verb tenses.

_____

_____

_____

_____

_____

_____

_____

E. Parse the following sentence in the space between the lines. Give the part of speech for every word. Give the case and reason for the case for every noun and adjective. Give the person, number, and tense of every verb.

Deinde Sabīnae ē casīs Rōmānōrum

passīs capillīs ēvolāvērunt;

parvulōs portāvērunt et patribus

frātribusque monstrāvērunt.

Lesson Twenty-Four

The *third conjugation* of verbs in Latin is a bit different from the first two conjugations. The infinitive of a third conjugation verb ends with *-ere*. *Dūcō, dūcere, dūxī, ductum* is a third conjugation verb.

Third conjugation verbs form their present stem by dropping *-ō* from the first principal part.

> ## Present Stem (3rd conj.) = First principal part *-ō*

To add the personal endings (*-ō, -s, -t, -mus, -tis, -nt*) directly to a consonant ending would make the words impossible to say, so we add *-i* or *-u* before the personal endings.

Here is the paradigm for third conjugation present tense verbs.

PRESENT

SINGULAR		PLURAL	
dūc*ō*	I lead	dūc*imus*	we lead
dūc*is*	you lead	dūc*itis*	you (pl.) lead
dūc*it*	he, she, it leads	dūc*unt*	they lead

The imperfect tense of third conjugation verbs is formed by adding the tense sign *-ēbā-* to the present stem.

Imperfect tense (3rd conj.) = present stem + ēbā + personal endings

---

Here is the paradigm for third conjugation imperfect tense verbs.

IMPERFECT

SINGULAR		PLURAL	
dūc*ēbam*	I was leading	dūc*ēbāmus*	we were leading
dūc*ēbās*	you were leading	dūc*ēbātis*	you (pl.) were leading
dūc*ēbat*	he, she, it was leading	dūc*ēbant*	they were leading

The future tense is formed by adding the tense sign *-ē-*, but pay close attention to the paradigm; *-ē-* becomes *-a-* in the first person singular and *-e-* before *-t* and *-nt* in the third person.

Future tense (3rd conj.) = present stem + ē + personal endings

---

Here is the paradigm for third conjugation future tense verbs.

FUTURE

SINGULAR		PLURAL	
dūc*am*	I will lead	dūc*ēmus*	we will lead
dūc*ēs*	you will lead	dūc*ētis*	you (pl.) will lead
dūc*et*	he, she, it will lead	dūc*ent*	they will lead

Lesson Twenty-Four Exercises

A. Study this new vocabulary.

contendō, -ere, -tendī, -tentum	to hasten, to hurry
dēfendō, -ere, -fendī, -fensum	to defend
dīcō, -ere, dīxī, dictum	to say
dūcō, -ere, dūxī, ductum	to lead
fallō, fallere, fefellī, falsum	to deceive, to escape the notice of
incolō, -ere, -uī	to inhabit, to dwell in
legō, -ere, lēgī, lectum	to read
mittō, mittere, mīsī, missum	to send
quaerō, quaerere, quaesīvī, quaesītum	to seek, to look for
regō, -ere, rēxī, rēctum	to rule
scrībō, -ere, scripsī, scriptum	to write
tegō, -ere, texī, tectum	to cover

B. Practice using third conjugation verbs in the three tenses you
have learned. Write equivalent phrases in Latin.

1. I will hurry _____

2. We will be able to read _____

3. They defend _____

4. She was deceiving _____

5. We will write _____

6. You (pl.) are seeking _____

7. He will lead _____

8. You (s.) were sending _____

9. They inhabit _____

10. He rules _____

11. They were saying _____

12. It will cover _____

13. We were defending _____

14. Do you (pl.) deceive? _____

15. Will they send? _____

C. Write ten excellent English sentences using words derived from this week's vocabulary.

1. _____

2. _____

3. _____

4. _____

5. _____

6. _____

7. _____

8. _____

9. _____

10. _____

DAILY ORAL REVIEW

Conjugate a verb from each of the three conjugations each day.

Decline a noun each day.

Review third declension vocabulary.

Lesson Twenty-Five

The *perfect system of the third conjugation* forms its tenses by the same rules as for the first and second conjugations. To find the perfect stem, drop the *-ī* from the third principal part. To form the perfect tense, add the perfect personal endings. To form the pluperfect tense, add the tense sign *-erā-* and the personal endings. To form the future perfect tense, add the tense sign *-eri-* and the personal endings.

Perfect tense = perfect stem + perfect endings

Perfect stem = third principal part *-ī*

This paradigm is for third conjugation perfect tense verbs.

PERFECT

SINGULAR		PLURAL	
dūx*ī*	I led, I have led	dūx*imus*	we led
dūx*istī*	you led	dūx*istis*	you (pl.) led
dūx*it*	he, she, it led	dūx*ērunt*	they led

> ## PluPerfect tense =
> ## perfect stem + erā + personal endings

This paradigm is for third conjugation pluperfect tense verbs.

PLUPERFECT

SINGULAR		PLURAL	
dūx*eram*	I had led	dūx*erāmus*	we had led
dūx*erās*	you had led	dūx*erātis*	you (pl.) had led
dūx*erat*	he, she, it had led	dūx*erant*	they had led

> ## Future Perfect tense =
> ## perfect stem + eri + personal endings

This paradigm is for third conjugation future perfect tense verbs.

FUTURE PERFECT

SINGULAR		PLURAL	
dūx*erō*	I will have led	dūx*erimus*	we will have led
dūx*eris*	you will have led	dūx*eritis*	you (pl.) will have led
dūx*erit*	he, she, it will have led	dūx*erint*	they will have led

Lesson Twenty-Five Exercises

A. Study this new vocabulary.

agō, agere, ēgī, āctum	to do, to drive
amittō, -ere, amīsī, amissum	to lose, to let go (ā+mittō)
cōgō, -ere, coēgī, coāctum	to collect; to compel (co+agō)
cōnstruō, -ere, -strūxī, -strūctum	to build, to construct
fluō, -ere, flūxī, flūxum	to flow
gerō, gerere, gessī, gestum	to bear, to wear
pōnō, pōnere, posuī, positum	to place, to put
relinquō, -ere, -relīquī, relictum	to leave, to leave behind
surgō, -ere, surrēxī, surrēctum	to rise, to stand up
vincō, vincere, vīcī, victum	to conquer, to defeat

B. Write a story about a past event. Try to use only third declension nouns and third conjugation verbs.

Lesson Twenty-Six

There is a second group of third conjugation verbs. These are called *third conjugation I-stem verbs*. These verbs are easily identified by their *-ere* infinitive ending and the *-i* in the present stem (which we find for this conjugation by dropping the *-ō* of the first principal part). The present system (present, imperfect, and future tenses) is only a little bit different from the other third conjugation verbs. The perfect system (perfect, pluperfect, and future perfect tenses) follows the rules exactly.

Here is the present system paradigm of a third conjugation I-stem verb.

SINGULAR		PLURAL	
PRESENT			
faciō	I make, I do	facimus	we make
facis	you make	facitis	you (pl.) make
facit	he, she, it makes	faciunt	they make
IMPERFECT			
faciēbam	I was making	faciēbāmus	we were making
faciēbās	you were making	faciēbātis	you (pl.) were making
faciēbat	he, she, it was making	faciēbant	they were making
FUTURE			
faciam	I will make, I will do	faciēmus	we will make
faciēs	you will make	faciētis	you (pl.) will make
faciet	he, she, it will make	facient	they will make

The perfect system of third conjugation verbs looks like this:

SINGULAR	PLURAL

PERFECT

fēc*ī*	I made, I have made	fēc*imus*	we have made
fēc*istī*	you have made	fēc*istis*	you (pl.) have made
fēc*it*	he, she, it has made	fēc*iērunt*	they have made

PLUPERFECT

fēc*eram*	I had made, I had done	fēc*erāmus*	we had made
fēc*erās*	you had made	fēc*erātis*	you (pl.) had made
fēc*erat*	he, she, it had made	fēc*erant*	they had made

FUTURE PERFECT

fēc*erō*	I will have made	fēc*erimus* we will have made
fēc*eris*	you will have made	fēc*eritis* you (pl.) will have made
fēc*erit*	he, she, it will have made	fēc*erint* they will have made

Lesson Twenty-Six Exercises

A. Study this new vocabulary.

accipiō, accipere, accēpī, acceptum	to receive, to accept (ad + capiō)
capiō, capere, cēpī, captum	to take, to capture
cōnficiō, -ficere, -fēcī, -fectum	to accomplish, to finish (cum + faciō)
cupiō, cupere, cupīvī, cupītum	to wish, to want, to desire
faciō, facere, fēcī, factum	to make, to do
fugiō, fugere, fūgī, fugitum	to flee, to flee from
iaciō, iacere, iēcī, iactum	to throw, to hurl
incipiō, incipere, incēpī, inceptum	to begin (in + capiō)

B. Tell why?

    1. a person would want to capture a confection?

    2. Cupid is the symbol of cupidity?

    3. a fact is something that is done?

    4. a fugitive is always on the run?

    5. to eject is to throw away?

    6. a plan may be doomed from its inception?

    7. a gift may be given, but it must also be accepted?

    8. insipid does not come from incipiō?

C. Give the Latin phrase which means the same thing as:

    1. We shall accomplish _____

    2. He has fled _____

    3. You (pl.) were throwing _____

    4. She shall have begun _____

    5. They were capturing _____

    6. He had begun _____

7. We wish _____

8. You have accomplished _____

9. They will capture _____

10. Am I accepting? _____

D. Read the story for enjoyment. Who had the last laugh?

BACCHUS ET PĪRĀTAE

Inter deōs Rōmānōs agricolae nōn sōlum Cererem sed Bacchum quoque adōrābant et in summō honōre habēbant. Bacchus enim vīnum hominibus dedit et multās artēs docuit. Ad Bacchī ārās agricolae dōna multa, et in prīmīs ūvās vīnumque iūcundum ferēbant, et ārās flōribus laetīs pampinīsque ornābant. Deus igitur vītēs Italicās cūrābat, et ā perīculō dēfendēbat. Formōsus erat deus, et, quod vītēs amābat, capillōs suōs pampinīs saepe ornābat. Nec Italōs Graecōsque sōlum docēbat, sed ad longinquās terrās nāvigābat, aliīsque gentibus vīnum dabat, artēsque rusticās docēbat.

Deus, ubi trāns mare Aegaeum quondam nāvigābat, ad insulam parvam nāvem gubernāvit, et errōribus longīs fessus, sē in ōrā maritimā prostrāvit et somnō placidō corpum animumque recreābat. Mox autem pīrātae quoque, hominēs malī, nāvem ad insulam impulērunt. Ubi iuvenem formōsum in ōrā vidērunt, tum vērō magnō gaudiō, "Ecce!" inquiunt, "nōn sine praedā ad patriam nostram nāvigābimus. Hominem raptābimus et in nāvem furtim impōnēmus, tum cito cum captīvō ad Africam nāvem impellēmus. Africae incolae servōs dēsīderant, et pecūniam multam nōbīs dābunt, sī nōs iuvenem tam pulchrum trādiderimus." Tum pīrātae, malī ignāvīque hominēs, deum raptāvērunt et in nāvem imposuērunt; nec tamen iuvenem fessum ē somnō excitāvērunt.

Ubi autem Bacchus ē somnō sē excitāvit, et undās caeruleās undique vīdit, tum nec īrātus nec perterritus, "Nōn egō," inquit, "stultōs ignāvōsque timeō; mox tamen pīrātae nūmen meum vidēbunt et vehementer timēbunt." Tum ē mediā nāve vītis flōrēbat et in altum ascendēbat. E vīte rāmī ē rāmīs pampinī flōrēbant, et dē summīs rāmīs ūvae purpureae pendēbant. Nōn iam candida erant vēla, sed lūce purpureā fulgēbant.

Ubi nautae vītem mīram in mediā nāve vīdērunt, tum magnō timōre deum spectāvērunt; capillī in capitibus horruērunt. Subitō ex undīs tigrēs leōnēsque saevī in nāvem ascendērunt et in nautās perterritōs cucurrērunt. Pīrātae, terrōris plēnī, ē nāve in mare sē prostrāvērunt. Deinde Iuppiter propter misericordiam hominēs in delphīnīs convērtit. Intereā Neptūnus vēla purpurea ventīs secundīs implēvit, et sōlus sub vitium umbrā Bacchus ad terrās longinquās nāvigāvit.

VERBS

horreō, -ēre, -uī, ---- —to shudder, to bristle
impellō, -ere, -pulī, -pulsum—to impel, to drive
trādō, -ere, -didī, -ditum—to hand over, to trade

NOUNS

delphīn, -īnis, n.—dolphin
error, -ōris, m.—wandering
leō, leōnis, m.—lion
misericordia, -ae, f.—pity
nūmen, -inis, n.—a divine power
pampinus, -ī, m.—a vine leaf or tendril

perīculum, -ī, n.—danger
praeda, -ae, f.—plunder
tigris, -is, m/f—tiger
vēlum, -ī, n.—sail
vītis, -is, f.—vine

ADJECTIVES

candidus, -a, -um—white
fessus, -a, -um—tired
saevus, -a, -um—savage, cruel

PRONOUNS

ego—I
nōbīs—to us
nōs—we

Optional Unit—Animals

Now that we have learned the third declension, our vocabulary can grow by leaps and bounds. Here are some animal and outdoor words which will be fun to use in compositions.

animal, -lis, n.	animal
arbor, -oris, f.	tree
avis, -is, f.	bird
bōs, bovis, m/f	ox, cow
delphīn, -īnis, n.	dolphin
grex, gregis, m.	flock
leo, leōnis, m.	lion
lux, lūcis, f.	light
mare, maris, n.	sea
mōns, montis, m.	mountain
nāvis, -is, f.	ship
nox, noctis, f.	night
ovis, ovis, m/f	sheep
pastor, -ōris, m.	shepherd
ramus, -ī, m.	branch
tigris, -is, m/f	tiger

Optional Unit—Animals Exercises

A. Tell me in Latin.

1. Three birds are sitting on the branch of a green tree.

2. A lion and a bear are fighting in the forest.

3. The tigers have killed a large white ox.

4. The horses were walking in front of a beautiful wagon.

5. The flock has begun to wander.

6. Animals have not always been fierce.

7. The sheep of the bad shepherd's flock stayed on the mountain all (use *tōtus*) night.

8. The ship sailed quickly through the waters of the sea.

9. It is night, and there is no light on the mountain or the sea.

10. The savage white lion fled from the small, strong man.

Paradigm Summaries

First Declension Nouns

CASE	SINGULAR	PLURAL
Nominative	puella	puellae
Genitive	puellae	puellārum
Dative	puellae	puellīs
Accusative	puellam	puellās
Ablative	puellā	puellīs

Masculine Second Declension Nouns

	SINGULAR	PLURAL
Nominative	amīcus	amīcī
Genitive	amīcī	amīcōrum
Dative	amīcō	amīcīs
Accusative	amīcum	amīcōs
Ablative	amīcō	amīcīs

Neuter Second Declension Nouns

	SINGULAR	PLURAL
Nominative	forum	fora
Genitive	forī	forōrum
Dative	forō	forīs
Accusative	forum	fora
Ablative	forō	forīs

Masculine and Feminine Third Declension Nouns

CASE	SINGULAR	PLURAL
Nominative	mīles	mīlitēs
Genitive	mīlitis	mīlitum
Dative	mīlitī	mīlitibus
Accusative	mīlitem	mīlitēs
Ablative	mīlite	mīlitibus

Neuter Third Declension Nouns

Nominative	caput	capita
Genitive	capitis	capitum
Dative	capitī	capitibus
Accusative	caput	capita
Ablative	capite	capitibus

Masculine and Feminine Third Declension I-stem Nouns

	SINGULAR	PLURAL
CASE		
Nominative	nox	noctēs
Genitive	noctis	noctium
Dative	noctī	noctibus
Accusative	noctem	noctēs
Ablative	nocte	noctibus

Neuter Third Declension I-stem Nouns

Nominative	mare	maria
Genitive	maris	marium
Dative	marī	maribus
Accusative	mare	maria
Ablative	marī	maribus

First Conjugation Verbs

	SINGULAR		PLURAL

PRESENT

vocō	I call	vocāmus	we call
vocās	you call	vocātis	you (pl.) call
vocat	he, she, it calls	vocant	they call

IMPERFECT

vocābam	I was calling	vocābāmus	we were calling
vocābās	you were calling	vocābātis	you (pl.) were calling
vocābat	he, she, it was calling	vocābant	they were calling

FUTURE

vocābō	I will call	vocābimus	we will call
vocābis	you will call	vocābitis	you (pl.) will call
vocābit	he, she, it will call	vocābunt	they will call

PERFECT

vocāvī	I called, I have called	vocāvimus	we called
vocāvistī	you called	vocāvistis	you (pl.) called
vocāvit	he, she, it called	vocāvērunt	they called

PLUPERFECT

vocāveram	I had called	vocāverāmus	we had called
vocāverās	you had called	vocāverātis	you (pl.) had called
vocāverat	he, she, it had called	vocāverant	they had called

FUTURE PERFECT

vocāverō	I will have called	vocāverimus	we will have called
vocāveris	you will have called	vocāveritis	you (pl.) will have called
vocāverit	he, she, it will have called	vocāverint	they will have called

Second Conjugation Verbs

Singular   Plural

Present

teneō	I hold	tenēmus	we hold
tenēs	you hold	tenētis	you (pl.) hold
tenet	he, she, it holds	tenent	they hold

Imperfect

tenēbam	I was holding	tenēbāmus	we were holding
tenēbās	you were holding	tenēbātis	you (pl.) were holding
tenēbat	he, she, it was holding	tenēbant	they were holding

Future

tenēbō	I will hold	tenēbimus	we will hold
tenēbis	you will hold	tenēbitis	you (pl.) will hold
tenēbit	he, she, it will hold	tenēbunt	they will hold

Perfect

tenuī	I held, I have held	tenuimus	we held
tenuistī	you held	tenuistis	you (pl.) held
tenuit	he, she, it held	tenuērunt	they held

PluPerfect

tenueram	I had held	tenuerāmus	we had held
tenuerās	you had held	tenuerātis	you (pl.) had held
tenuerat	he, she, it had held	tenuerant	they had held

Future Perfect

tenuerō	I will have held	tenuerimus	we will have held
tenueris	you will have held	tenueritis	you (pl.) will have held
tenuerit	he, she, it will have held	tenuerint	they will have held

Third Conjugation Verbs

SINGULAR   PLURAL

PRESENT

dūcō	I lead	dūcimus	we lead
dūcis	you lead	dūcitis	you (pl.) lead
dūcit	he, she, it leads	dūcunt	they lead

IMPERFECT

dūcēbam	I was leading	dūcēbāmus	we were leading
dūcēbās	you were leading	dūcēbātis	you (pl.) were leading
dūcēbat	he, she, it was leading	dūcēbant	they were leading

FUTURE

dūcam	I will lead	dūcēmus	we will lead
dūcēs	you will lead	dūcētis	you (pl.) will lead
dūcet	he, she, it will lead	dūcent	they will lead

PERFECT

dūxī	I led, I have led	dūximus	we led
dūxistī	you led	dūxistis	you (pl.) led
dūxit	he, she, it led	dūxērunt	they led

PLUPERFECT

dūxeram	I had led	dūxerāmus	we had led
dūxerās	you had led	dūxerātis	you (pl.) had led
dūxerat	he, she, it had led	dūxerant	they had led

FUTURE PERFECT

dūxerō	I will have led	dūxerimus	we will have led
dūxeris	you will have led	dūxeritis	you (pl.) will have led
dūxerit	he, she, it will have led	dūxerint	they will have led

Third Conjugation I-stem Verbs

	SINGULAR		PLURAL

PRESENT

faciō	I make, I do	facimus	we make
facis	you make	facitis	you (pl.) make
facit	he, she, it make	faciunt	they make

IMPERFECT

faciēbam	I was making	faciēbāmus	we were making
faciēbās	you were making	faciēbātis	you (pl.) were making
faciēbat	he, she, it was making	faciēbant	they were making

FUTURE

faciam	I will make, I will do	faciēmus	we will make
faciēs	you will make	faciētis	you (pl.) will make
faciet	he, she, it will make	facient	they will make

PERFECT

fēcī	I made, I have made	fēcimus	we have made
fēcistī	you have made	fēcistis	you (pl.) have made
fēcit	he, she, it has made	fēcērunt	they have made

PLUPERFECT

fēceram	I had made, I had done	fēcerāmus	we had made
fēcerās	you had made	fēcerātis	you (pl.) had made
fēcerat	he, she, it had made	fēcerant	they had made

FUTURE PERFECT

fēcerō	I will have made	fēcerimus	we will have made
fēceris	you will have made	fēceritis	you (pl.) will have made
fēcerit	he, she, it will have made	fēcerint	they will have made

Irregular Verb - Sum

	SINGULAR			PLURAL

PRESENT

sum	I am	sumus	we are
es	you are	estis	you (pl.) are
est	he, she, it is	sunt	they are

IMPERFECT

eram	I was	erāmus	we were
erās	you were	erātis	you (pl.) were
erat	he, she, it was	erant	they were

FUTURE

erō	I will be	erimus	we will be
eris	you will be	eritis	you (pl.) will be
erit	he, she, it will be	erunt	they will be

PERFECT

fuī	I was, I have been	fuimus	we have been
fuistī	you have been	fuistis	you (pl.) have been
fuit	he, she, it has been	fuērunt	they have been

PLUPERFECT

fueram	I had been	fuerāmus	we had been
fuerās	you had been	fuerātis	you (pl.) had been
fuerat	he, she, it had been	fuerant	they had been

FUTURE PERFECT

fuerō	I will have been	fuerimus	we will have been
fueris	you will have been	fueritis	you will have been
fuerit	he, she, it will have been	fuerint	they will have been

Irregular Verb - Possum

	SINGULAR		PLURAL

PRESENT

possum	I can, I am able	possumus	we are able
potes	you are able	potestis	you (pl.) are able
potest	he, she, it is able	possunt	they are able

IMPERFECT

poteram	I was able, I could	poterāmus	we were able
poterās	you were able	poterātis	you (pl.) were able
poterat	he, she, it was able	poterant	they were able

FUTURE

poterō	I will be able	poterimus	we will be able
poteris	you will be able	poteritis	you (pl.) will be able
poterit	he, she, it will be able	poterunt	they will be able

PERFECT

potuī	I was able, I have been able	potuimus	we have been able
potuistī	you have been able	potuistis	you (pl.) have been able
potuit	he, she, it has been able	potuērunt	they have been able

PLUPERFECT

potueram	I had been able	potuerāmus	we had been able
potuerās	you had been able	potuerātis	you (pl.) had been able
potuerat	he, she, it had been able	potuerant	they had been able

FUTURE PERFECT

potuerō	I will have been able	potuerimus	we will have been able
potueris	you will have been able	potueritis	you will have been able
potuerit	he, she, it will have been able	potuerint	they will have been able

First and Second Declension Adjectives

Singular

	Masculine	Feminine	Neuter
Nominative	bonus	bona	bonum
Genitive	bonī	bonae	bonī
Dative	bonō	bonae	bonō
Accusative	bonum	bonam	bonum
Ablative	bonō	bonā	bonō

Plural

	Masculine	Feminine	Neuter
Nominative	bonī	bonae	bona
Genitive	bonōrum	bonārum	bonōrum
Dative	bonīs	bonīs	bonīs
Accusative	bonōs	bonās	bona
Ablative	bonīs	bonīs	bonīs

Third Declension Adjectives

SINGULAR

	MASCULINE/FEMININE	NEUTER
Nominative	viridis	viride
Genitive	viridis	viridis
Dative	viridī	viridī
Accusative	viridem	viride
Ablative	viridī	viridī

PLURAL

	MASCULINE/FEMININE	NEUTER
Nominative	viridēs	viridia
Genitive	viridium	viridium
Dative	viridibus	viridibus
Accusative	viridēs	viridia
Ablative	viridibus	viridibus

Latin Vocabulary

Vocabulary–Nouns and Pronouns

A

Africa, -ae, f.,	Africa
ager, -rī, m.,	field, land
agricola, -ae, m.,	farmer
amīcus, -ī, m.,	friend
amita, -ae, f.,	aunt
angulus, -ī, m.,	corner
animus, -ī, m.,	mind
annus, -ī, m.,	year
Apūlia, -ae, f.,	Apulia, a district of Italy
aqua, -ae, f.,	water
āra, -ae, f.,	altar
arbor, -oris, f.,	tree
arma, -ōrum, n. pl.,	arms
armentum, -ī, n.,	herd
ars, artis, f.,	art
audācia, -ae, f.,	boldness
auxilium, auxiliī, n.,	help, aid, assistance
avāritia, -ae, f.,	greed
avia, -ae, f.,	grandmother
avus, -ī, m.,	grandfather

B

Bacchus, -ī, m.,	Bacchus, the god of the vine
bellum, -ī, n.,	war
benevolentia, -ae, f.,	favor, good will
bēstia, -ae, f.,	wild beast
bōs, bovis, m./f.,	ox
bracchium, -ī, n.,	arm
Britannia, -ae, f.,	Britain
Britannus, -ī, m.,	a Briton

C

caelum, -ī, n.,	sky

campus, -ī, m.,	plain
Campus Martius	a strip of land near the Tiber River where the Romans met
capillus, -ī, m.,	hair
captīvus, -ī, m.,	captive
caput, capitis, n.,	head
carmen, -inis, n.,	song
casa, -ae, f.,	house, cottage
causa, -ae, f.,	cause
cēna, -ae, f.,	dinner
Cerēs, Cereris, f.,	Ceres, goddess of the corn
cibus, -ī, m.,	food
cicāda, -ae, f.,	grasshopper
cīvis, -is, m./f.,	citizen
cīvitas, -ātis, f.,	state
clīvus, -ī, m.,	hill
collum, -ī, n.,	neck
columba, -ae, f.,	dove
coma, -ae, f.,	hair
constantia, -ae, f.,	constancy, steadfastness
cōpia, -ae, f.,	supply, abundance
cor, cordis, n.,	heart
corona, -ae, f.,	crown
corpus, -oris, n.,	body
cūnae, -ārum, f. pl.,	cradle
cūra, -ae, f.,	care, worry

D

dea, -ae, f.,	goddess
deus, -ī, m.,	god
dextra, -ae, f.,	right hand
dictum, -ī, n.,	saying
dōnum, -ī, n.,	gift
duodecim	twelve

E

eques, -itis, m.,	horseman, knight
equus, -ī, m.,	horse
error, -ōris, m.,	wandering

F

fābula, -ae, f.,	story, tale, fable
factum, -ī, n.,	deed
fāma, -ae, f.,	fame, talk, rumor, report
familia, -ae, f.,	household
famula, -ae, f.,	a female servant, handmaid
fēmina, -ae, f.,	woman
fenestra, -ae, f.,	window
figūra, -ae, f.,	shape, figure
fīlia, -ae, f.,	daughter
flamma, -ae, f.,	flame
flōs, flōris, m.,	flower
focus, -ī, m.,	hearth
folium, -ī, n.,	leaf
forum, -ī, n.,	forum, market place
fragor, -oris, m.,	crash
frāter, -ris, m.,	brother
frūmentum, -ī, n.,	corn
fulmen, -inis, n.,	lightning, thunder-bolt

G

galea, -ae, f.,	helmet
gaudium, -ī, n.,	joy
gemma, -ae, f.,	gem, jewel
gens, gentis, f.,	race
genu, -ūs, n.,	knee
gladius, -ī, m.,	sword
Graecus, -ī, m.,	a Greek
gremium, -ī, n.,	lap
grex, gregis, m.,	flock

H

harēna, -ae, f.,	beach, sand
hasta, -ae, f.,	spear
herba, -ae, f.,	herb, plant
hiems, -emis, f.,	winter
homo, -inis, m./f.,	a man, human being
honor, -ōris, m.,	honor
hōra, -ae, f.,	hour
Horātius, -ī, m.,	Horatius, a brave Roman

I

ianua, -ae, f.,	door
īra, -ae, f.,	wrath, anger
imber, -ris, m.,	rain, shower
incola, -ae, m.,	inhabitant, resident, settler
infans, -fantis, m./f.,	infant
Inferī, ōrum, m.pl.,	the Lower World
insula, -ae, f.,	island
īra, -ae, f.,	anger
Ītalia, -ae, f.,	Italy
Ītalus, -ī, m.,	an Italian
iter, itineris, n.,	journey
Iūlia, -ae, f.,	Julia
Iūlius, -ī, m.,	Julius, a Roman
Iuppiter, Iovis, m.,	Jupiter, king of the gods
iūs, iūris, n.,	law, justice
iuvencus, -i, m.,	bullock
iuvenis, -is, m./f.,	a young man or woman

L

lacerta, -ae, f.,	lizard
lacrima, -ae, f.,	tear
lacūna, -ae, f.,	pool, pond
latebra, -ae, f.,	hiding place, lair, hideout
lectus, -ī, m.,	bed, couch

liber, -rī, m.,	book
līberī, -ōrum, m. pl.,	children
līlium, -ī, n.,	lily
lingua, -ae, f.,	tongue, language
littera, -ae, f.,	letter (of the alphabet)
litterae, -ārum, f. pl.,	letter (correspondence)
locus, -ī, m.,	place
lūcerna, -ae, f.,	lantern, lamp
lūdus, -ī, m.,	play, school
lūna, -ae, f.,	moon
lupus, -ī, m.,	wolf

M

magister, -rī, m.,	teacher, master
mare, -is, n.,	sea
Mars, Martis, m.,	Mars, god of war
māter, -ris, f.,	mother
memoria, -ae, f.,	memory
mensa, -ae, f.,	table
Metanīra, -ae, f.,	Metanira, mother of Triptolemus
mīles, -itis, m./f.,	soldier
monumentum, -ī, n.,	monument
Mūsae, -ārum, f. pl.,	Muses, nine goddesses

nāvicula, -ae, f.,	small ship or boat
nāvis, -is, f.,	ship
nauta, -ae, m.,	sailor
nepos, nepōtis, m.,	grandson
neptis, neptis, f.,	granddaughter
nōs	we
nūmen, -inis, n.,	a divine power
nympha, -ae, f.,	nymph

O

oculus, oculī, m.,	eye
olīva, -ae, f.,	olive
onus, -eris, n.,	burden, load

oppidānus, -ī, m.,	a townsman
oppidum, -ī, n.,	town
ōra, -ae, f.,	coast, shore
ōra maritima, -ae, f.,	sea shore
orbis, -is, m.,	circle
orbis terrārum	the whole world
osculum, -ī, n.,	kiss

P

palla, -ae, f.,	cloak
pampinus, -ī, m.,	a vine leaf or tendril
parens, -entis, m./f.,	parent
pater, -ris, m.,	father
patria, -ae, f.,	fatherland, country
patruus, -ī, m.,	uncle
pectus, -oris, n.,	breast
paenīnsula, -ae, f.,	peninsula
pax, pācis, f.,	peace
pecūnia, -ae, f.,	money, reward
perīculum, -ī, n.,	danger
Persephonē, -ēs, f.,	Persephone, daughter of Ceres
pēs, pedis, m.,	foot
pīrāta, -ae, f.,	pirate
pictūra, -ae, f.,	picture
plaustrum, -ī, n.,	wagon
Plūto, -ōnis, m.,	Pluto, king of the Underworld
poēta, -ae, m.,	poet
poena, -ae, f.,	penalty, punishment
pōmum, -ī, n.,	fruit, apple
pontus, -ī, m.,	sea
populus, -ī, m.,	people, nation
porta, -ae, f.,	door, gate
praeda, -ae, f.,	plunder
prandium, -ī, n.,	lunch
prātum, -ī, n.,	meadow
proelium, proeliī, n.,	battle, fight
prōra, -ae, f.,	prow

prōvincia, -ae, f.,	province
puella, -ae, f.,	girl
puer, -ī, m.,	boy

Q

Quirīnus, -ī, m.,	Quirinus, the name of Romulus after he was deified
Quirītēs, -ium, m.pl.,	Quirites, a name of the Roman people

R

rēgīna, -ae, f.,	queen
rēgia, -ae, f.,	palace, royal residence
regio, -ōnis, f.,	region, district
regnum, -ī, n.,	kingdom
rex, rēgis, m.,	king
rīpa, -ae, f.,	bank (of a river)
Rōma, -ae, f.,	Rome
Rōmānus, -ī, m.,	a Roman
Rōmulus, -ī, m.,	Romulus, the founder of Rome
rosa, -ae, f.,	rose
rota, -ae, f.,	wheel
ruīna, -ae, f.,	ruin
rūs, rūris, n.,	country

S

Sabīnus, -ī, m.,	a Sabine, neighbor of the Romans
sagitta, -ae, f.,	arrow
sapientia, -ae, f.,	wisdom
saxum, -ī, n.,	rock, stone
schola, -ae, f.,	school
scūtum, -ī, n.,	shield
sē	himself, etc (*reflexive pronoun*)
semita, -ae, f.,	path
servus, -ī, m.,	slave
Sicilia, -ae, f.,	Sicily
silva, -ae, f.,	forest, wood

sinistra, -ae, f.,	left hand
sinistrum, -ī, n.,	left side
somnus, -ī, m.,	sleep
soror, -ōris, f.,	sister
stella, -ae, f.,	star

T

tabula, -ae, f.,	tablet
templum, -ī, n.,	temple
tempus, -oris, n.,	time
tenebrae, -ārum, f. pl.,	shadows, darkness
terra, -ae, f.,	land, earth, ground
Tiberis, -is, m.,	the Tiber River
timor, -ōris, m.,	fear
toga, -ae, f.,	toga, the dress of the Roman men
Triptolemus, -ī, m.,	Triptolemus, the inventor of agriculture
tunica, -ae, f.,	tunic
turba, -ae, f.,	crowd, throng, mob

U

umbra, -ae, f.,	shade, shadow, ghost
unda, -ae, f.,	wave
urbs, urbis, f.,	city
ursa, -ae, f.,	bear
ursus, -ī, m.,	bear
ūva, -ae, f.,	grape
uxor, -ōris, f.,	wife

V

vallis, -is, f.,	valley
ventus, -ī, m.,	wind
verbum, -ī, n.,	word
via, -ae, f.,	street, road, highway, way, journey
victima, -ae, f.,	victim
villa, -ae, f.,	villa, house
vīnea, -ae, f.,	vineyard

vīnum, -ī, n.,	wine
vir, -ī, m.,	man, hero, husband
virgo, -inis, f.,	virgin
vīta, -ae, f.,	life
vītis, -is, f.,	vine
vōs	you (*plural*)
vox, vōcis, f.,	voice

Vocabulary–Adjectives and Adverbs

A

ā sinistrā	on the left hand
adhūc	still, yet
adolescens, adolescentis	young, just grown up
Aegaeus, Aegaea, Aegaeum	Aegaean
aeger, aegra, aegrum	sick
albus, alba, album	white
alius, alia, alium	another
altus, alta, altum	high, deep
amoenus, amoena, amoenum	pleasant, lovely
apertus, aperta, apertum	open
armātus, armāta, armātum	armed

B

bene	well
benignus, benigna, benignum	kind
bonus, bona, bonum	good
Britannicus, Britannica, Britannicum	British

C

caeruleus, caerulea, caeruleum	blue
cārus, cāra, cārum	dear
celeriter	quickly
cēteri, cēterae, cētera	the rest
citō	quickly
cotīdiē	every day
croceus, crocea, croceum	yellow
crūdēliter	cruelly

D

deinde	then, next
dīligenter	carefully
dēnsus, dēnsa, dēnsum	thick, dense
diū	for a long time
dīvīnus, dīvīna, dīvīnum	divine

E

etiam	even, also
extrēmus, extrēma, extrēmum	extreme, farthest

F

ferendus, ferenda, ferendum	bearable, to be borne
ferus, fera, ferum	fierce
fessus, fessa, fessum	tired
fīdus, fīda, fīdum	faithful
fīnitimus, fīnitima, fīnitimum	neighbouring
firmus, firma, firmum	firm, strong
flāvus, flāva, flāvum	yellow, yellow-haired
formōsus, formōsa, formōsum	beautiful
fortasse	perhaps
forte	by chance
fortiter	bravely
frustrā	in vain
furtim	secretly, stealthily

G

grātus, grāta, grātum	pleasing
gelidus, gelida, gelidum	cold
grātus, grāta, grātum	pleasant, welcome

H

herbōsus, herbōsa, herbōsum	grassy
hic	here

I

iam	now, already
ibi	there
ignāvus, ignāva, ignāvum	cowardly, base
ignōtus, ignōta, ignōtum	unknown
impavidus, impavida, impavidum	fearless
industrius, industria, industrium	industrious
intereā	meanwhile

īrātus, īrāta, īrātum	angry
iterum	again
iūcundus, iūcunda, iūcundum	pleasant

L

laetus, laeta, laetum	happy, glad
lātus, lāta, lātum	wide, broad
lībenter	willingly, gladly
līberus, lībera, līberum	free
longinquus, longinqua, longinquum	distant
longus, longa, longum	long

M

maestus, maesta, maestum	sad
magnus, magna, magnum	great, large
malus, mala, malum	bad, evil, wicked
māne	in the morning
Martius, Martia, Martium	belonging to Mars
medius, media, medium	middle
meus, mea, meum	my
mīrus, mīra, mīrum	wonderful
miser, misera, miserum	unhappy
mox	soon
multus, multa, multum	many, much

N

nōn	not
nōn iam	no longer
noster, nostra, nostrum	our
nōtus, nōta, nōtum	well known, famous
nullus, nulla, nullum	no
nunc	now
nusquam	nowhere

O

ōlim	one day, once upon a time

P

placidus, placida, placidum	calm
parātus, parāta, parātum	ready
parvulus, parvula, parvulum	little
parvus, parva, parvum	small, little
passim	everywhere
passus, passa, passum	spread out, dishevelled
perterritus, perterrita, perterritum	frightened
piger, pigra, pigrum	lazy
plēnus, plēna, plēnum	full
prīmus, prīma, prīmum	first
praeclārus, praeclāra, praeclārum	splendid, famous
procul	far
profundus, profunda, profundum	deep
pulcher, pulchra, pulchrum	beautiful
purpureus, purpurea, purpureum	purple

Q

quiētus, quiēta, quiētum	quiet
quondam	once upon a time
quoque	also

R

raucus, rauca, raucum	noisy, raucous
rectus, recta, rectum	straight, right
Rōmānus, Rōmāna, Rōmānum	Roman
rotundus, rotunda, rotundum	round
ruber, rubra, rubrum	red
rusticus, rustica, rusticum	rustic, belonging to the country

S

Sabīnus, Sabīna, Sabīnum	Sabine
saepe	often
saevus, saeva, saevum	savage, cruel
satis	enough
scelerātus, scelerāta, scelerātum	wicked
semper	always
serēnus, serēna, serēnum	calm

sollicitus, sollicita, sollicitum	anxious
sōlus, sōla, sōlum	alone, only
splendidus, splendida, splendidum	splendid
statim	at once
stultus, stulta, stultum	foolish
subitō	suddenly
summus, summa, summum	highest, very great
suus, sua, suum	his own (*reflexive adjective*)

T

tandem	at last
tōtus, tōta, tōtum	whole
tum	then
tuus, tua, tuum	thy, your (*singular*)

U

ubi	where, when (*relative adverb*)
undique	on every side, from all sides
ūnus, ūna, ūnum	one

V

validus, valida, validum	strong
vehementer	exceedingly, very much
vērō	indeed
vester, vestra, vestrum	your (*plural*)

Vocabulary–Verbs

A

accusō, -āre, -āvī, -ātum	to accuse, to blame
adōrō, -āre, āvī, -ātum	to worship
aedificō, -āre, āvī, -ātum	to build
agitō, -āre, -āvī, -ātum	to drive, to arouse, to disturb
ambulō, -āre, -āvī, -ātum	to walk
amō, -āre, -āvī, -ātum	to love
apportō, -āre, -āvī, -ātum	to bring, to take
appropinquō, -āre, -āvī, -ātum	to approach, to draw near
arō, -āre, -āvī, -ātum	to plough

C

cantō, -āre, -āvī, -ātum	to sing
cēlō, -āre, -āvī, -ātum	to hide, to conceal
clāmō, -āre, -āvī, -ātum	to shout, to cry out
conciliō, -āre, - āvī, -ātum	to win over
conservō, -āre, -āvī, -ātum	to save, to preserve
contendō, -ere, -tendī, -tentum	to hasten
convocō, -āre, -āvī, -ātum	to call together
culpō, -āre, -āvī, -ātum	to blame
cūrō, -āre, -āvī, -ātum	to take care of

D

dēfendō, -ere, -fendī, -fensum	to defend
dēlectō, -āre, -āvī, -ātum	to delight
dēmonstrō, -āre, -āvī, -ātum	to point out, to show
dēsiderō, -āre, -āvī, -ātum	to desire, to want
dō, dare, dedī, datum	to give
doceō, -ere, docuī, doctum	to teach
dormītō, -āre, -āvī, -ātum	to sleep

E

ecce	behold
errō, -āre, -āvī, -ātum	to err, to wander, to be mistaken
excidō, -ere, -cīdī, -cīsum	to cut down, to destroy

exclāmō, -āre, -āvī, -ātum	to exclaim
exerceō, -ere, -cuī, -citum	to exercise
expectō, -āre, -āvī, -ātum	to expect, to wait for
explorō, -āre, -āvī, -ātum	to explore
ēvocō, -āre, -āvī, -ātum	to evoke, to call forth
ēvolō, -āre, -āvī, -ātum	to fly out

F

fallō, -ere, fefelli, falsum	to deceive, to escape the notice of
ferō, ferre, tuli, lātum	to bear, to carry
fleō, -ēre, flēvi, flētum	to weep
flōreō, -ēre, -ruī	to flourish, to flower
fugō, -āre, -āvī, -ātum	to put to flight
fulgeō, -ēre, fulsī	to shine

G

gubernō, -āre, -āvī, -ātum	to govern, to steer

H

habeō, -ēre, -buī, -bitum	to have, to hold
habitō, -āre, -āvī, -ātum	to dwell, to live in, to inhabit
horreō, -ēre, -uī, -itum	to shudder, to bristle

I

iaceō, -ēre, -cuī	to lie
iaceo, iacere, iēcī, iactum	to lay, to throw
iactō, -āre, -āvī, -ātum	to throw, to toss
impellō, -ēre, -pulī, -pulsum	to impel, to drive
impōnō, -ēre, -posuī, -positum	to put in or on
incitō, -āre, -āvī, -ātum	to urge on
incolō, -ēre, -uī	to inhabit, to dwell in
inquit	said he
inquiunt	said they
invītō, -āre, -āvī, -ātum	to invite
iuvō, iuvāre, iūvī, iūtum	to help, to aid

L

labōrō, -āre, -āvī, -ātum	to work
lacrimō, -āre, -āvī, -ātum	to weep
laudō, -āre, -āvī, -ātum	to praise
laxō, -āre, -āvī, -ātum	to relax, to loosen
legō, -ēre, lēgī, lectum	to read

M

mactō, -āre, -āvī, -ātum	to offer up, to slay
mandō, -āre, -āvī, -ātum	to entrust
maneō, -ēre, mansī, mansum	to remain
monstrō, -āre, -āvī, -ātum	to show, to point out
mutō, -āre, -āvī, -ātum	to change, to alter

N

nārrō, -āre, -āvī, -ātum	to narrate, to tell
natō, -āre, -āvī, -ātum	to swim
navigō, -āre, -āvī, -ātum	to sail
necō, -āre, -āvī, -ātum	to kill
nominō, -āre, -āvī, -ātum	to name, to call

O

occupō, -āre, -āvī, -ātum	to seize, to occupy
ornō, -āre, -āvī, -ātum	to adorn, to equip
orō, -āre, -āvī, -ātum	to ask for
oppugnō, -āre, -āvī, -ātum	to attack

P

parō, -āre, -āvī, -ātum	to prepare
perterreō, -ēre, -uī, -itum	to frighten
portō, -āre, -āvī, -ātum	to carry
postulō, -āre, -āvī, -ātum	to demand
properō, -āre, -āvī, -ātum	to hasten, to hurry
prosternō, -ere, -strāvī, -strātum	to prostrate, to overthrow
pugnō, -āre, -āvī, -ātum	to fight

Q

quaerō, -ere, -sīvī, -sītum	to seek, to look for

R

raptō, -āre, -āvī, -ātum	to snatch, to seize
recitō, -āre, -āvī, -ātum	to read aloud, to recite
recreō, -āre, -āvī, -ātum	to refresh
recūsō, -āre, -āvī, -ātum	to refuse
regnō, -āre, -āvī, -ātum	to reign
rogō, -āre, -āvī, -ātum	to ask

S

saltō, -āre, -āvī, -ātum	to dance
scibō, -ēre, scripsi, scriptum	to write
sedeō, -ēre, sēdī, sessum	to sit
servō, -āre, -āvī, -ātum	to save, to keep
spectō, -āre, -āvī, -ātum	to look at, to watch
stō, stare, stetī, statum	to stand
sum, esse, fuī, futurus	to be

T

tardō, -āre, -āvī, -ātum	to slow down, to delay
tegō, -ēre, texī, tectum	to cover
temptō, -āre, -āvī, -ātum	to try, to attempt
teneō, -ēre, tenuī, tentum	to hold
timeō, -ēre, -uī	to fear
trādō, -ēre, -idī, -itum	to hand over

V

valē, *pl.* valēte	goodbye
valeō, -ēre, valuī	I am well
videō, -ēre, vīdī, vīsum	to see
vigilō, -āre, -āvī, -ātum	to be on guard, to stand watch
vitō, -āre, -āvī, -ātum	to avoid, to shun
vocō, -āre, -āvī, -ātum	to call
volō, -āre, -āvī, -ātum	to fly
vulnerō, -āre, -āvī, -ātum	to wound

Vocabulary–Conjunctions and Prepositions

A

ā, ab	by, from
ad	to, towards
ante	before
autem	but

C

cum	with

E

et	and
et . . . et	both . . . and
ē, ex	out of, from

D

dē	down from, concerning

I

igiter	therefore
in *(with ablative)*	in, on
in *(with accusative)*	into, onto
in prīmis	especially
inter	between, among
ita	so, thus
itaque	and so

N

nam	for
nec	and not, nor
neque	and not, nor

P

per	through, among
post	after

prō	for, on behalf of
prope	near
propter	on account of

Q

-que	and
quia	because
quod	because

S

sed	but
sī	if
sine	without

T

tam	so
tamen	however
trans	across